# HOW AN ECONOMY GROWS *and* WHY IT DOESN'T

by IRWIN A. SCHIFF

Art by VIC LOCKMAN

## BOOKS BY IRWIN SCHIFF

The Great Income Tax Hoax

How An Economy Grows and Why It Doesn't

The Social Security Swindle — How Anyone Can Drop Out

How Anyone Can Stop Paying Income Taxes

The Kingdom of Moltz

The Biggest Con: How The Government Is Fleecing You


Published by Freedom Books
P.O. Box 5303, Hamden, Connecticut 06518



Library of Congress Cataloging Card No. 85-070522
ISBN: 0-930374-06-1

Dedicated to
Adam Smith,
who, in his book
"Wealth of Nations" 1776,
laid a foundation for the
science of economics
which is in sharp contrast
to the voodoo economics
now being preached in
this nation's capitol.

HOW an ECONOMY GROWS
A FISH STORY
ONCE UPON AN ISLAND LIVED THREE MEN WHO FISHED FOR FOOD EVERY DAY...
I'M ABLE!
I'M BAKER!
AND I'M CHARLIE!
UGH! FISHING BY HAND IS NO BUCKET OF BASS!
IT'S HARDER THAN EATING SOUP WITH A FORK!
BUT AFTER MUCH TROUBLE THEY EACH MANAGED TO CATCH ONE FISH PER DAY...

AND EVERY DAY ABLE, BAKER AND CHARLIE CONSUMED THE FISH EACH HAD CAUGHT, ENABLING THEM TO SURVIVE TO THE NEXT DAY TO CATCH ANOTHER FISH...

ANOTHER DAY... ANOTHER FISH!
SLURP!
BURP!

THIS IS **SURVIVAL,** AND THAT'S ABOUT ALL...

Z

AND SO, IN THIS SUPER SIMPLE ISLAND SOCIETY THERE ARE...

NO SAVINGS
NO CREDIT!
NO INVESTMENT!

EVERYTHING THAT IS PRODUCED IS CONSUMED!

ONE NIGHT, LOOKING UP INTO THE STAR-STUDDED SKY, ABLE IS STRUCK BY A THOUGHT...
THERE MUST BE MORE TO LIFE THAN CATCH, EAT AND CATCH!
THERE IS!
HIS THINK-BOX STARTED GRINDING...
AND THE IDEA FOR A FISH-CATCHER IS BORN...
I'LL CALL IT A NET!
SO, THE NEXT DAY...
I NEED NET MATERIALS!
WHAT?! YOU'RE NOT GOING FISHING TODAY, ABLE?!
YOU'LL GO HUNGRY!

ABLE IS LIVING OUT A FEW VERY BASIC ECONOMIC PRINCIPLES IN ORDER TO IMPROVE HIS WAY OF LIFE...
HE IS UNDERCONSUMING and HE IS TAKING A RISK!
I'M GIVING UP SOMETHING ...EATING!
GROWL!
IT MIGHT NOT EVEN WORK!
AT DAY'S END ABLE HAS COMPLETED HIS NET! HE HAS CREATED CAPITAL THROUGH HIS SELF SACRIFICE!
WHEW!
HIS FRIENDS SNOOZE CONTENTEDLY TOWARD A NEW DAY OF HAND FISHING...
Z
Z
WHILE ABLE CAN'T SLEEP FOR HUNGER AND WORRY ABOUT HIS RISK TAKING EXPERI-MENT...

THE NEXT DAY BAKER AND CHARLIE MAKE MUCH SPORT OF ABLE'S INVENTION
YOU COULD WEAR IT LIKE A HAT...
YOU COULD TIE IT IN A BOW! HO-HO!
I'M GOING FISHING! YOU'LL SEE!
THE LAUGHS SOON FADE TO GASPS...
GASP! HE CAUGHT ONE ALREADY!
BRAVO! IT WORKS JUST AS I'D PLANNED!
AND BY DAY'S END ABLE HAS CAUGHT 2 FISH ...BAKER AND CHARLIE EACH THE USUAL
I'M DEAD TIRED, TOO!
NOW I HAVE 1 MORE FISH THAN I NEED TO CONSUME ...I HAVE GENERATED SAVINGS!

# ABLE'S SAVINGS CREATE CAPITAL

SINCE THE ISLAND SOCIETY HAD NO STORE OF SAVINGS THE ISLAND'S FIRST PIECE OF **CAPITAL EQUIPMENT** WAS DERIVED SOLELY FROM ABLE'S WILLINGNESS TO DENY HIMSELF FOOD FOR **1** DAY!
NOW I DON'T HAVE TO SPEND EVERY DAY **FISHING!**
NOW I HAVE TIME TO BUILD A BETTER SHELTER, MAKE TOOLS AND TILL THE SOIL!

**WITHOUT A SUPPLY OF SAVINGS (CAPITAL) AN ECONOMY *CANNOT GROW!***

BAKER AND CHARLIE SOON REALIZE THAT THEY TOO COULD BENEFIT FROM ABLE'S NET... HIS CAPITAL!
HEY, ABLE, OL' BUDDY-BUDDY...
LET US BORROW YOUR NET, HUH?
BUT ABLE IS NOBODY'S FOOL! HE REMEMBERS HIS SELF SACRIFICE...
HUNGER...
...RISK!
NOTHING DOING! MAKE YOUR OWN NET, BUDDY-BUDDIES!
HUH? B-BUT WE CAN'T STAND TO BE HUNGRY!
NOT EVERY-BODY IS CUT-OUT FOR SELF DEPRI-VATION!

BESIDES, WE'RE ALL THUMBS WHEN IT COMES TO HAND-CRAFT!
WE MIGHT STARVE TO DEATH BEFORE WE CAN MAKE A DECENT NET!
SO HOW ABOUT THIS... LOAN US SOME OF YOUR SURPLUS FISH TO EAT WHILE WE MAKE A NET?
WE'LL REPAY YOU FROM OUR NET CATCHES!
OH, YEAH! THEN IF YOU FAIL I'VE LOST MY SAVINGS!
I'D HAVE EVERYTHING TO LOSE AND NOTHING TO GAIN BY MAKING SUCH A LOAN!
HE'S GOT A POINT!
A STRAIGHT LOAN IS NO INCENTIVE FOR HIM!

BAKER AND CHARLIE'S THINK-BOXES MESH GEARS...
... AND A FINANCIAL IDEA IS BORN!
INTEREST
HEY, ABLE... HEAR THIS!
FOR EVERY FISH YOU LOAN TO US WHILE WE BUILD A NET WE'LL PAY BACK TWO FISH!
NOW THAT INTERESTS ME!
IF I LOAN THEM FOUR FISH I'LL GET BACK EIGHT FISH!
I'LL BE FOUR FISH RICHER WITHOUT DOING ANY MORE WORK!

# TWO-WAY BENEFITS

BUT IT'S NOT ONLY ABLE THE "CAPITAL-IST" WHO GAINS...
THIS DEAL REALLY WON'T COST US ANYTHING, CHARLIE!
YES, WE CAN USE ABLE'S CAPITAL WITHOUT ANY PERSONAL SACRIFICE...LIKE GOING HUNGRY!
WITH THE FOUR FISH WE BORROW WE CAN EAT WHILE BUILDING OUR NETS!
AND WITH OUR DAILY CATCH DOUBLED WE CAN SOON REPAY THE 4 FISH LOAN PLUS 4 FISH INTEREST TO ABLE!
IT'LL REALLY COST US NOTHING BECAUSE WE'LL PAY OFF ABLE OUT OF OUR IN-CREASED PRODUC-TIVITY, THANKS TO HIS SAVINGS!
WE'LL BE MUCH BETTER OFF AND SOON WE'LL HAVE CAPITAL SAVINGS TO LOAN OUT, TOO!

# ABLE'S SAVINGS OPTIONS

1 HE SIMPLY MIGHT HOLD ONTO HIS SAVINGS FOR POSSIBLE FUTURE *EMERGENCY USE,* BUT OF COURSE, *THEN THEY WOULDN'T GROW*...
ONCE *SMOKED* THEY DON'T SPOIL! I MIGHT WANT TO EAT THEM IF I'M EVER SICK OR SOMETHING HAPPENS!
2 HE COULD INDULGE HIMSELF AND **CONSUME** ALL HIS SAVINGS...
MAN, WHAT A PIG-OUT!
3 HE COULD LOAN OUT HIS FOUR FISH TO BAKER AND CHARLIE AND GET BACK EIGHT FISH IF THEY SUCCEEDED IN BUILDING NETS!
**RISK** REARS ITS UGLY HEAD!
≡ULP!≡ IF THEY FAIL I'VE *LOST MY SAVINGS!*

4 BUT STILL ANOTHER POSSIBILITY STRUCK ABLE...
INSTEAD OF LOANING FISH (CONSUMPTION GOODS) TO BAKER AND CHARLIE TO SUSTAIN THEMSELVES WHILE THEY BUILD A NET (A CAPITAL GOOD), WHY NOT USE THE FISH MYSELF?

I'LL CONSUME ONE FISH PER DAY FOR TWO DAYS WHILE I BUILD TWO MORE NETS...

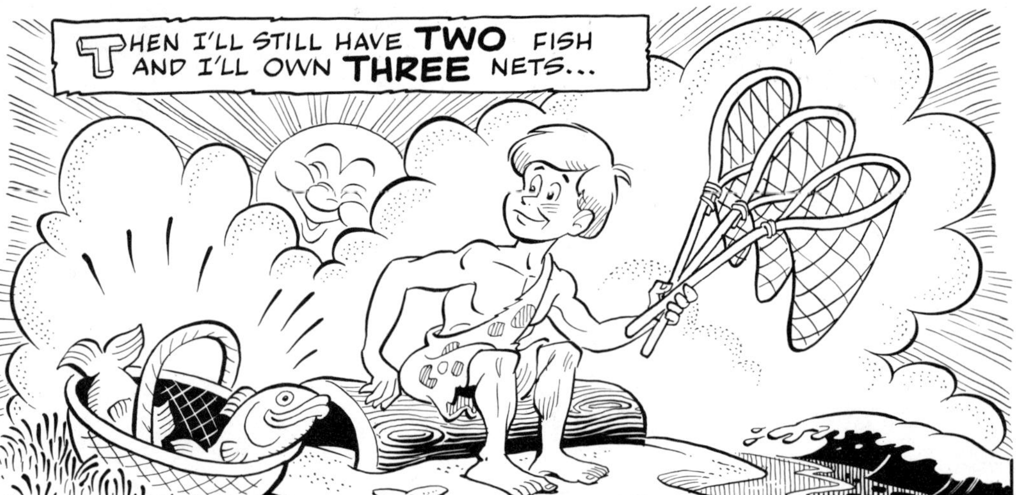
THEN I'LL STILL HAVE TWO FISH AND I'LL OWN THREE NETS...

NEXT, I CAN RENT A NET TO BAKER AND CHARLIE FOR 1/2 A FISH PER DAY, A REASONABLE FEE...
BAKER AND CHARLIE WILL EACH BE ABLE TO CATCH TWO FISH PER DAY WITH THE NETS!
SINCE I WOULD'VE CAUGHT 1 FISH WITHOUT THE NET, AND SUBTRACTING 1/2 FISH RENT... I'M NOW 1/2 FISH RICHER!
IT BEATS THE HARD WORK OF HAND-FISHING WHEREBY I CAN CATCH ONLY 1 FISH PER DAY!
... AND I CAN RETIRE AND NEVER WORK AGAIN, WITH 30 FISH PER MONTH RENTAL FEES COMING IN!

IT BEATS LOANING 4 FISH TO BAKER AND CHARLIE TO BUILD THEIR OWN NETS! THAT WOULD HAVE EARNED ME A TOTAL OF ONLY 4 FISH!
OF COURSE BAKER AND CHARLIE MIGHT ONLY RENT THE NETS FOR 2 DAYS... THEN USE THEIR SAVINGS TO BUILD NETS FOR THEMSELVES...I'D BE ONLY 2 FISH AHEAD!

WHAT TO DO?.... LOAN OUT 4 FISH, SO BAKER AND CHARLIE CAN BUILD THEIR OWN NETS, AND GET 8 FISH BACK, OR...EAT TWO OF MY FISH WHILE BUILDING 2 MORE NETS FOR RENTAL THAT MIGHT BRING BACK ONLY 2 FISH... BUT POSSIBLY STEADY RETIREMENT EARNINGS?
DECISIONS...DECISIONS! BUT NO MATTER WHICH WAY HE GOES, IF BAKER AND CHARLIE ARE SUCCESSFUL, ABLE WILL HAVE INCREASED HIS AND SOCIETY'S CAPITAL!

Review
ABLE (AND SOCIETY) HAS ONLY FIVE THINGS HE CAN DO WITH HIS SAVINGS GAINED BY SELF-SACRIFICE...
1
HE CAN SAVE WHAT HE HAS SAVED
2
HE CAN CONSUME WHAT HE HAS SAVED
3
HE CAN LOAN OUT WHAT HE HAS SAVED...
LOANS
WE'VE GOT FOOD...LET'S TAKE A DAY TO BUILD NETS!
4
HE CAN INVEST WHAT HE HAS SAVED...
5
OR HE CAN TRY A COMBINATION OF ALL FOUR CHOICES

WHATEVER ABLE DOES IT WILL BE BASED UPON THE RELATIVE RISK AND PROFIT REWARDS & HIS PERSONAL ECONOMIC NEEDS!
SAVINGS OPTIONS
1. SAVE SAVINGS
2. CONSUME
3. LOAN OUT
4. INVEST
5. COMBINATION
WE'LL TELL YOU WHAT TO DO WITH YOUR CAPITAL, ABLE...
?
LOAN IT OUT FOR LOW-LOW INTEREST!
HOW ABOUT CHARITY? DIVVY UP!
OR HOW ABOUT THIS?!
OH, NO YOU DON'T!
I'M THE ONLY ONE WHO STANDS TO LOSE DIRECTLY IF MY SAVINGS ARE WASTED!
SLAM!
MORAL RIGHT
SO ONLY ABLE HAS THE MORAL AND EQUITABLE RIGHT TO DECIDE HOW TO USE HIS PROPERTY!

WHATEVER CHOICE ABLE MAKES EVENTUALLY WILL ENABLE THE COMMUNITY TO GENERATE 3 EXTRA FISH PER DAY, ASSUMING THEY ALL CONTINUE TO WORK JUST AS HARD!

WHAT ABOUT GREED?
WON'T IT BE BAD IF ABLE TURNS OUT TO BE A GREEDY GUY, WANTING MORE AND MORE WEALTH?
BAD FOR WHO?
THE ONLY WAY ABLE'S WEALTH CAN INCREASE IS IF HE MAKES HIS WEALTH AVAILABLE TO OTHER MEMBERS OF THE COMMUNITY!
EQUIPMENT RENTAL
FISH LOANS
OTHERWISE HIS WEALTH WILL STAY THE SAME OR GET SMALLER AS HE PERSONALLY USES IT UP!
THE NOBLE THING ABOUT PRIVATE CAPITALISM IS THAT IT FORCES THOSE WHO MAY ONLY BE MOTIVATED BY PERSONAL GAIN TO RAISE THE STANDARD OF LIVING OF OTHERS!
CAPITAL

SO ABLE DECIDES TO LOAN 4 FISH TO BAKER & CHARLIE...
NOW WE HAVE FISH TO EAT WHILE WE BUILD OUR OWN NETS!
THE NETS ARE MADE...
AND THEY NOW CATCH ENOUGH FISH TO EAT AND TO PAY BACK THEIR LOAN TO ABLE...
NOW ABLE HAS PROFITED FROM HIS LOAN, AND SO HAVE BAKER AND CHARLIE...
I'M 4 FISH RICHER!
WE OWN NETS WE DIDN'T OWN BEFORE!

EXPANSION
NOW BAKER AND CHARLIE FISH FOR A FULL WEEK, SAVING ENOUGH FISH TO ENABLE THEM TO DEVOTE ANOTHER WEEK'S EFFORT ON A STILL BIGGER CAPITAL PROJECT...
MONDAY
TUESDAY
WED.
THURS.
FRIDAY
SAT.
THIS MUCH LARGER PROJECT REQUIRES MORE AND NEW MATERIALS...PLUS INGENUITY...
LET'S BUILD A BIGGER AND BETTER FISH CATCHER!
WE NEED TOUGHER STUFF... LIKE VINES!
...AND BAMBOO!

# the BETTER FISH TRAP

OUR BIG TRAP CATCHES FISH CONTINUALLY!
OUTSIDE OF A FEW REPAIRS NOW AND THEN, WE ONLY HAVE TO GATHER THE FISH WE WANT TO EAT EACH DAY...PLUS SOME EXTRAS TO SAVE!
NOW WE HAVE PLENTY TO EAT AND LOTS OF LEISURE WITH SAVINGS TO BOOT!
WE DON'T HAVE A CARE IN THE WORLD!
OH, NO?
HUH? WHAT DO YOU KNOW ABOUT THE FISH BUSINESS, OWL?
I KNOW PLENTY ABOUT DISASTERS, CHUMP!

# NATURAL DISASTERS... ACTS OF GOD

THESE MAY DISRUPT THE ISLAND'S ECONOMY BY DAMAGING ITS CAPITAL...THE BIG FISH TRAP.

THE FLOOD HAS DESTROYED OUR TRAP!
THERE GO MY SAVINGS!

BUT WHEN WE FIND "HARD TIMES" (SUCH AS RECESSION AND DEPRESSION) IN THE ABSENCE OF NATURAL DISASTERS, THEIR CAUSE IS MAN-MADE!

# UNNATURAL DISASTERS

THROUGHOUT HISTORY *UNNATURAL DISASTERS* HAVE BEEN CAUSED BY NONPRODUCTIVE POLITICIANS MEDDLING IN THE NATURAL ECONOMIC ORDER TO STEAL THE PRODUCTIVITY OF SOME FOR THE BENEFIT OF OTHERS.

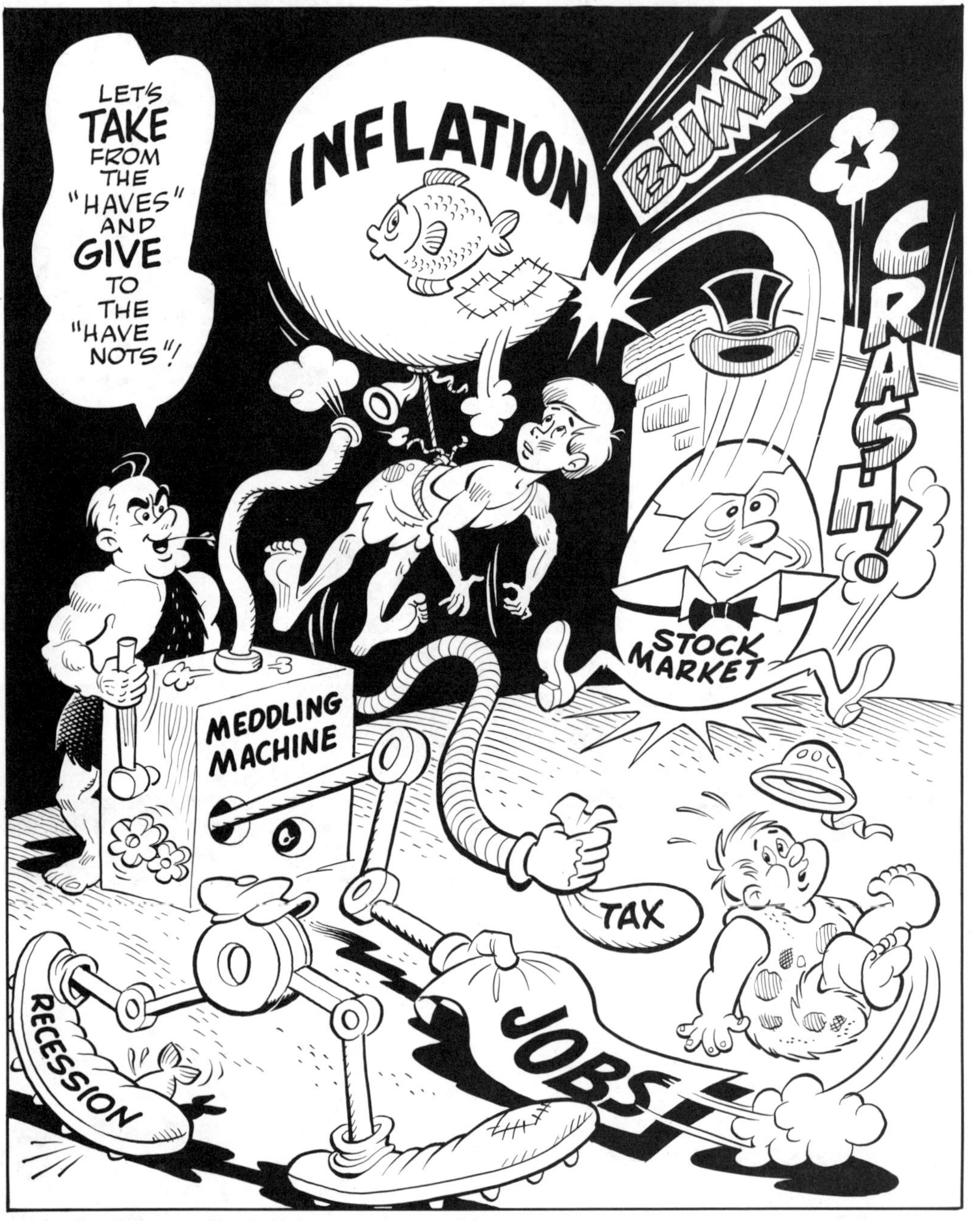

ISLAND CONSUMER DEBT
SUPPOSE BAKER AND CHARLIE APPROACHED ABLE FOR A "VACATION LOAN" INSTEAD OF A LOAN FOR BUILDING NETS...
WE'RE TIRED AND NEED A REST!
LOAN US EACH TWO FISH SO WE CAN BASK ON THE BEACH A FEW DAYS!
IT WILL COST YOU EACH 2 FISH IN INTEREST! HOW WILL YOU REPAY?
ER...WE'LL WORK HARDER!
AND DO WITHOUT EATING FOR SEVERAL DAYS!
YOU'LL HAVE TO GO WITHOUT EATING 4 DAYS TO REPAY YOUR LOAN!
BUT WE'VE JUST GOTTA HAVE A VACATION!

LOOK! WHY BORROW AND GO HUNGRY 4 DAYS TO RE-PAY THE LOAN, WHEN WITHOUT BORROWING YOU CAN FINANCE YOUR VACATION BY GOING WITH-OUT FISH FOR ONLY 2 DAYS?
GIVE ME ONE GOOD REASON!
WE WANNA TAKE OUR VACATION
NOW!
YIKES! THE "NOW" ORIENTED GENERATION!
I DENY YOUR LOAN WHICH WOULD ONLY BENEFIT ME AND BE AN ECONOMIC BURDEN TO YOU!
BESIDES... IF I MAKE A CONSUMER LOAN TO YOU I WON'T HAVE AS MUCH TO LOAN OUT FOR PRODUCTIVE PURPOSES!
BAH! FOOEY!

CAN ABLE EXPAND CREDIT?
HOCUS POCUS!
POLITICIANS AND BANKERS FREQUENTLY REFER TO "EXPANDING" OR "EASING" OF CREDIT! BUT CAN ANYBODY DO THIS AT COMMAND?
CAN A STATIST MAGICIAN REALLY MAKE MORE WEALTH AVAILABLE TO LOAN BY A MERE WAVE OF HIS MAGIC WAND?
THE OBVIOUS ANSWER IS NO!
NOBODY CAN LOAN OUT SOMETHING THEY DON'T HAVE! ANY ATTEMPT TO DO SO IS TRICKERY and FRAUD!
TAKE THIS! I'LL MAKE GOOD ON IT!
10 FISH
WHO ARE YOU KIDDIN' !?!
YOU HAVE ONLY 4 FISH IN YOUR BASKET!
LOANS

THE ISLAND'S TOTAL SUPPLY OF CREDIT IS LIMITED BY ITS TOTAL SUPPLY OF FISH!

# the EMERGENCY LOAN for CONSUMPTION

ABLE HAS WISELY REJECTED BAKER AND CHARLIE'S REQUEST FOR A "VACATION" (CONSUMPTION) LOAN, AND A WEEK LATER...
BAKER AND CHARLIE CANNOT FISH BECAUSE OF A STORM OR SICKNESS...
OOH!

NOW, OUT OF COMPASSION, ABLE MAKES A CONSUMER LOAN OUT OF HIS SACRIFICIALLY ACCUMULATED SAVINGS SO THAT BAKER AND CHARLIE CAN EAT AND LIVE TO WORK ANOTHER DAY...

LOANS
THANKS, ABLE!
WE'LL WORK HARD AND SCRIMP AND SAVE TO PAY YOU BACK!

BUT SUPPOSE ABLE HAD GRANTED THE ORIGINAL & NEEDLESS

# CONSUMPTION LOAN FOR A VACATION

BAKER AND CHARLIE SQUANDER THE ISLAND'S SAVINGS HAVING FUN ON THE BEACH...
EASY COME...
EASY GO!
AND THEN A STORM STRIKES
WHO TURNED OUT THE SUN ?
YIKES! HEAD FOR A CAVE!
HURRY! IT'S A HURRICANE!

THE STORM RAGES FOR DAYS, MAKING FISHING IMPOSSIBLE!
DON'T YOU HAVE ANY MORE FISH, ABLE?
SORRY! YOU WASTED ALL THE ISLAND'S SAVINGS VACATIONING!
IN THEIR WEAKENED CONDITION DISEASE COULD TAKE OVER...
RESULT... THE ISLAND SOCIETY COULD BE TOTALLY WIPED-OUT, THANKS TO "CONSUMER DEBT." THE GREAT WASTER!
ABLE RIP
BAKER RIP
CHARLIE RIP

# SURVIVAL OF THE SAVERS

IF ON THE OTHER HAND, ABLE REFUSED TO MAKE THE "VACATION LOAN," HE WOULD HAVE HAD "EMERGENCY FUNDS" AVAILABLE TO WEATHER THE STORM...
WE CAN GET BY ON LESS BECAUSE WE'RE NOT USING UP ENERGY WORKING!
WE'LL SURVIVE... THANKS TO ABLE'S SAVINGS!
A DEPRESSION OR A RECESSION HAS SET IN!

YES, SAVINGS CAN MEAN THE DIFFERENCE BETWEEN THE LIFE AND DEATH OF SOCIETY!

LESSON:
CONSUMPTION LOANS WASTE SAVINGS
INVESTMENT OR CAPITAL LOANS TEND TO INCREASE SAVINGS
Loan
Interest
Increase
+
=

LIFE
SAVINGS
IT MAKES A BIG DIFFERENCE
DEATH
CONSUMER DEBT

# CAPITAL LOAN RISK

OF COURSE, NOT ALL INVESTMENTS OR CAPITAL LOANS WORK OUT, AND THIS CAN ALSO BRING ABOUT A REDUCTION AND A WASTE OF SOCIETY'S STORE OF SAVINGS! BUT THE ONES THAT WORK MAKE UP FOR THE ONES THAT DON'T!

ABLE MAY HAVE MADE LOANS TO BAKER AND CHARLIE TO BUILD NETS, BUT...
I'M A POOR NET-MAKER!
WHERE ARE ALL THE FISH TODAY?
OR ABLE MAY HAVE USED UP HIS CAPITAL BUILDING MORE NETS FOR HIMSELF, BUT...
I CAN'T FIND ENOUGH SUPPLIES! UGH!
I NEED THIS FOR MY NEST!
BAKER AND CHARLIE IRRATIONALLY REFUSE TO RENT MY NETS!

# 2 BIG LESSONS

**1** LOANS FOR ***CONSUMPTION*** PURPOSES REDUCE THE AMOUNT OF FUNDS AVAILABLE TO FINANCE BOTH ***CAPITAL*** *PROJECTS* AND THE PRODUCTION OF MORE ***CONSUMER*** GOODS, AND THEREFORE CAN ONLY ***LOWER*** SOCIETY'S STANDARD OF LIVING AND ITS ECONOMIC SECURITY.

HI-HO...HI-HO...IT'S OFF FOR FUN WE GO...
I'M OUT OF FUNDS NOW!
FUN LOANS
NO SURF-BOARDS?
SURF
I COULDN'T BORROW TO BUILD 'EM!
NO SUN-GLASSES!
WHY NOT?
FOOLS!
YOUR CONSUMPTION LOANS TOOK ALL OF THE ISLAND'S SAVINGS SO THAT NO LOANS WERE AVAILABLE FOR MANUFACTURING SURFBOARDS, SUN-GLASSES, OR ANY-THING ELSE!

**2** GOVERNMENT PROGRAMS ENCOURAGING LOANS TO POOR QUALITY AND HIGH RISK APPLICANTS DEVELOP A HIGHER DEGREE OF CAPITAL FAILURE, AND WASTE SOCIETY'S SAVINGS IN THE SAME WAY AS GRANTING CONSUMER CREDIT!

GO AHEAD...LOAN TO THOSE POOR RISKS! I'LL GUARANTEE THE LOANS!
BUT GOVERNMENT HAS NO SAVINGS! IT CAN ONLY RAID THE SAVINGS OF THOSE WHO HAVE SACRIFICIALLY UNDER-CONSUMED TO CREATE SAVINGS!
GOV'T.
LOANS

# ENTER the BULLY

BUT NOW LET US SUPPOSE, THAT, WHILE BAKER AND CHARLIE WERE ATTEMPTING TO NEGOCIATE A CONSUMER LOAN FROM ABLE FOR A VACATION **FRANKLIN DEE** THE ISLAND'S BULLY SHOWED UP...

WHAT'S UP, CHUMS?
AW, ABLE WON'T MAKE A *VACATION LOAN* TO US!
LOANS
HE'S *STINGY!*
HE'S *GREEDY!*
SOB!
HE'S DENYING US A *MUCH NEEDED VACATION!*
BAW!
WHY, *YOU TIGHTWAD!* YOU'VE GOT **FOUR** *FISH* YOU *DON'T NEED;* SO WHY *DON'T* YOU *LOAN 'EM* TO *THESE GUYS?!*

MY SAVINGS REALLY AREN'T SAFE ANY MORE...NOT WITH THAT BULLY AROUND!
ANYBODY ELSE NEED A LOAN?

AFTER THIS I'M NOT GOING TO WORK SO HARD, NOR SACRIFICE AS MUCH TO SAVE!
WHAT'S THE USE?

TODAY, IN AMERICA, THE INFLUENCE OF POLITICIANS ON LOANING INSTITUTIONS OPERATES IN MUCH THE SAME WAY AS FRANKLIN DEE, TO:

1. WASTE SAVINGS BY ENCOURAGING THE UNECONOMIC USE OF *CREDIT*

2. DISCOURAGE SAVINGS BY *REDUCING* IF NOT *COMPLETELY ELIMINATING THE REWARDS OF THRIFT*

# the ISLAND ECONOMY GROWS

NOW LET'S SEE HOW THE ***SAME ECONOMIC RULES*** THAT OPERATE IN A ***SIMPLE*** ECONOMIC SOCIETY ALSO APPLY TO A MORE ***COMPLICATED*** ONE...

ABLE'S INITIAL WILLINGNESS TO CREATE CAPITAL THROUGH HIS OWN PERSONAL SACRIFICE HAS BENEFITED MANY OTHER ISLANDERS.
NOW THERE ARE MANY "ABLES" FISHING WITH THEIR OWN NETS...
BUT NOT EVERYBODY HAS THE SKILLS OF NETMAKING AND FISHING...
SOME ISLANDERS BORROW FISH TO SUSTAIN THEMSELVES WHILE THEY BUILD THE TOOLS OF OTHER TRADES...
I'M A HAMMOCK MAKER!
THERE'S LOTS OF NEED FOR WAGONS!
I MAKE TABLES AND CHAIRS!

I'M A (PUFF-PUFF!) BOULEVARD BUILDER!
ROUTE 1
AND THERE ARE ALSO BUILDING-BUILDERS...
OUTSTRETCHED ARMS APTS.
BOAT BUILDERS...
BUGGY BUILDERS...
BUGGY WORKS
PUFF-MOBILE

YOU NAME IT!
BRUSHES

THE ISLANDERS CONTINUED TO USE FISH AS A MEDIUM OF EXCHANGE. ALL WAGES AND PRICES WERE QUOTED IN TERMS OF SO MANY FISH; AS WERE THE TERMS OF LOANS. AND SINCE EACH PERSON ON THE ISLAND CONSUMED ONE FISH PER DAY, THE ISLAND'S PRICE STRUCTURE WAS RELATED TO THEIR DAILY CONSUMPTION OF FISH!

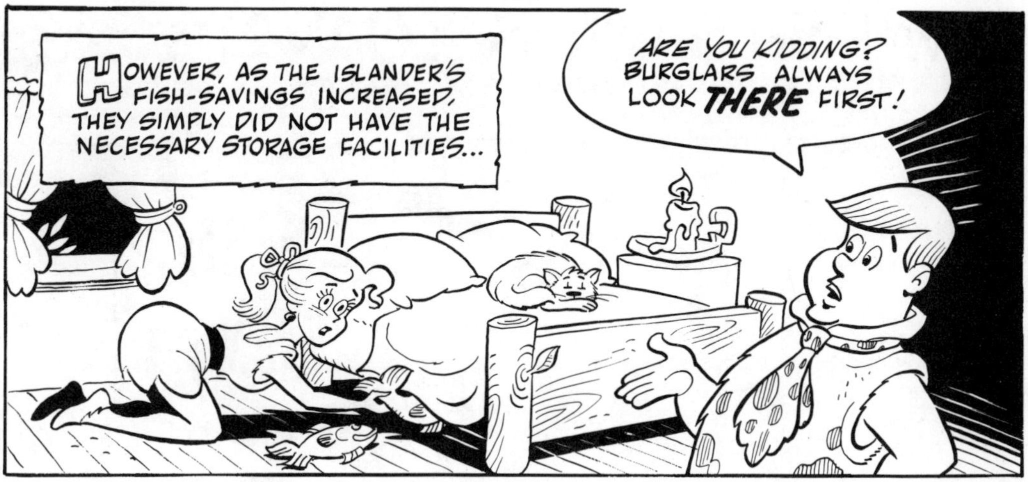
HOWEVER, AS THE ISLANDER'S FISH-SAVINGS INCREASED, THEY SIMPLY DID NOT HAVE THE NECESSARY STORAGE FACILITIES...
ARE YOU KIDDING? BURGLARS ALWAYS LOOK **THERE** FIRST!

AND WHILE THEY WOULD HAVE LIKED TO SEE THEIR SAVINGS GROW BY LOANS AND INVESTMENTS, INDIVIDUAL PRODUCERS HAD NEITHER THE TIME NOR TRAINING TO JUDGE THE MERITS OF BUSINESS PROPOSITIONS OFFERED TO THEM...

MARTHA, HE'S SELLING SHARES IN THE COD LIVER OIL SWEEP-STAKES!

SO, AN HONEST AND WISE MEMBER OF THE ISLAND COMMUNITY, **MAX GOODBANK,** SEEING A VERY REAL BUSINESS OPPORTUNITY, ENTERS THE SCENE...

I'LL BUILD A LARGE STORAGE FACILITY FOR THE ISLAND'S FISH SAVINGS!
JUST WHAT WE NEED!
ER...BUT JUST HOW WILL IT WORK?
COMMERCE

# How "FISH SAVINGS & LOAN Co works

WHEN THE "ABLES" OF THE ISLAND *UNDERCONSUME* THEY *DEPOSIT* THEIR *FISH SAVINGS WITH MR. GOODBANK...*

*SO THE ABLES DELEGATE INVESTMENT RESPONSIBILITY TO MR. GOODBANK!*

NOW THOSE REQUIRING CONSUMPTION GOODS (FISH) IN ORDER TO FINANCE A CAPITAL PROJECT NEED ONLY SEE MR. GOODBANK, RATHER THAN ALL OF THE "ABLES" ON THE ISLAND...
I NEED SOME FISH TO EAT WHILE I BUILD A TOOL FACTORY!
HMM... YOU HAVE A GOOD RECORD!
MR. GOODBANK HAS TOO MUCH INTEGRITY TO RISK THE ISLANDER'S SAVINGS ON VACATION LOANS AND THE LIKE...
BERMUDA
SORRY!
UNDER HIS WISE AND CONSERVATIVE CARE THE ISLAND'S SAVINGS AND COMMERCE CONTINUE TO GROW...
AIR CARGO

BUT MR. GOODBANK DOES HAVE COMPASSION FOR THOSE IN DESPERATE NEED OF CONSUMER CREDIT DUE TO DIRE EMERGENCY, POOR HEALTH, UNEMPLOYMENT, ETC.
I'VE SET UP A CONTINGENCY FUND FOR BORROWERS LIKE YOU, MR. HARDTIMES!
ZZZ
I'LL DO MY BEST TO REPAY THIS LOAN, SIR!
FISH SAVINGS AND LOAN CO
BUT IF BORROWERS ARE UNABLE TO PAY BACK THESE LOANS THE BULK OF THE ISLAND'S SAVINGS IS STILL UNTOUCHED AND AVAILABLE FOR ESSENTIAL ISLAND PROJECTS!
AFTER SAN FRANCISCO'S GREAT EARTHQUAKE IN 1906 A LOCAL BANKER MADE STREET CORNER EMERGENCY LOANS TO EARTHQUAKE VICTIMS...
EMERGENCY LOANS
LOW INTERE

NOW SEVERAL GENERATIONS HAVE PASSED SINCE THE ORIGINAL I.M. ABLE MADE HIS PERSONAL SACRIFICE AND CREATED THE ISLAND'S FIRST PIECE OF *CAPITAL EQUIPMENT* (A NET). THE ISLAND'S ECONOMIC AND SOCIAL PROGRESS BEGAN AT THAT POINT!
FISH
THE ISLAND CONTINUED TO DEVELOP AND PROSPER WITH MR. GOODBANK'S STORAGE VAULT AND HIS AND HIS SONS' WISE ADMINISTRATION OF LOANING OUT SOCIETY'S CAPITAL.
INVESTMENT DECISIONS CONTINUED TO BE MADE BY INDIVIDUALS...
LET'S PUT OUR FISH IN THE BANK!
FISH
LOAN DECISIONS WERE MADE BY MR. GOODBANK III
(HE LOOKS JUST LIKE HIS GRANDFATHER, DOESN'T HE?)
LOAN DENIED!
LOAN APPROVED!

# Enter Manny Fund

BUT SOME INVESTERS WANTED TO TAKE GREATER RISKS FOR POTENTIALLY GREATER REWARDS
?
NO, NO... TOO RISKY! I WON'T CHANCE IT!
WHY DON'T YOU LOAN TO THE NEWLY FORMED SLING-FLIGHT CO.?
IF THAT VENTURE REALLY FLIES WE'LL CLEAN UP!
MR. GOODBANK, TRUE TO FORM, WILL NOT INVEST IN HIGH RISK VENTURES!
AHEM! I BELIEVE I CAN BE OF SERVICE, GENTS!
HUH? WHO ARE YOU?
MANNY FUND IS THE NAME! POOL YOUR RISK CAPITAL WITH ME, AND I'LL INVEST THOSE SAVINGS IN HIGHER RISK VENTURES!
YAY! BIG PROFITS COMING! WE HOPE!
IT'LL BE WORTH THE RISK! HEY, GUYS...

SO, WHILE MR. GOODBANK CONTINUES TO BE ENTRUSTED WITH CAPITAL GROWTH THROUGH MORE *CONSERVATIVE* FORMS OF INVESTMENT, MANNY FUND INVESTS FOR THE RISK-TAKERS...
**H'RAY!** "SLING-FLIGHT" PROFITS ARE SOAR-ING!
FLIGHTS EVERY 5 MINUTES
DEPOT

BLUB!
BUT THE **"BLUBMARINE** COMPANY" *WENT UNDER!*
BLUBMARINE PORT
AND SO, THE ISLAND'S ECONOMY CONTINUES TO *GROW* TO THE BENEFIT OF *ALL!*

# the WATER SUPPLY PROBLEM

FROM THE BEGINNING ISLANDERS DREW THEIR WATER FROM THE MOUNTAIN STREAM...
SO MOST PEOPLE DIDN'T LIVE OR WORK VERY FAR FROM THE WATER SUPPLY!

ONE YEAR A DREADFUL DROUGHT, A NATURAL DISASTER, JUST ABOUT WIPED OUT EVERYBODY...
WHAT COULD BE DONE AS INSURANCE AGAINST SUCH A THING IN THE FUTURE?

THE FERTILE MIND OF "$H_2O$ PEDDLER" TACKLED THE PROBLEM...
HMM...IN NATURE RAIN RUNOFF COLLECTS IN PONDS! LET'S COPY NATURE!
LET'S BUILD A BIG RESERVOIR TO COLLECT AND SAVE RAIN WATER FOR FUTURE USE!
BLUE PRINT
MR. GOODBANK HAD A RECEPTIVE EAR!
AND EQUALLY IMPORTANT, THE ISLAND'S SAVINGS WERE NOW GREAT ENOUGH TO FUND SUCH A LARGE PROJECT...
THEN WE'LL CONSTRUCT A NETWORK OF PIPELINES, ETC., ETC...
YOU'VE GOT A LOAN FOR YOUR PROJECT, MR. $H_2O$ PEDDLER!
BLUE PRINT

# the WATER WORKS PROJECT

the WATER WORKS PROJECT REQUIRED AN INVESTMENT BY THE SAVERS OF THE COMMUNITY OF 547,500 FISH ...ENOUGH TO SUPPORT A CREW OF 250 MEN FOR 2 YEARS WHILE THEY LABORED...
BLUE PRINT
THE RISK WAS WEIGHED AGAINST SUCCESS! THE PROJECT, IF SUCCESSFUL, WOULD PAY FOR ITSELF AND INSURE A BETTER FUTURE FOR EVERY ISLANDER!

# the SPLASHING SUCCESS

OF THE WATERWORKS PROJECT FLOWED THROUGH THE ISLAND'S ECONOMY! PIPELINES, AVAILABLE FOR A REASONABLE CHARGE, BROUGHT WATER GREAT DISTANCES!

THIS BEATS HIKING UP TO "PRECIPICE POND"!
INDUSTRY & WORKERS COULD LOCATE AT POINTS REMOTE FROM THE SOURCE OF WATER.

IRRIGATION MADE CROP FAILURES LESS LIKELY...

RELIEVED OF THE TASK OF HAULING WATER BY HAND, EVERYBODY NOW HAS MORE TIME AND ENERGY TO DEVOTE TO PRODUCING MORE CONSUMER GOODS AND DEVELOPING NEW CAPITAL PROJECTS!
Productivity

THE WATER WORKS PROSPERED AND PAID BACK IT'S LOAN PLUS INTEREST. SO THE ISLAND'S SAVINGS CAPITAL GREW AND GREW UNDER MR. GOODBANK'S WATCHFUL CARE!
QUITE A CATCH!
WATER WORKS
SAVINGS AND LOAN CO.

THE ENTIRE ISLAND ECONOMY "BLOSSOMS" THANKS TO THE CAPITAL INVESTED IN THE WATER WORKS!

# BIG vs. LITTLE ECONOMICS

TO SOME ISLANDERS IT APPEARS THAT THE ECONOMICS OF PROSPERITY AND DISASTER HAVE BECOME DIFFERENT WITH BIGNESS AND COMPLEXITY FROM THOSE OF A SMALL ECONOMY...
WOW! IT'S A WHOLE *NEW* BALL OF WAX... OR BOX OF GEARS!
BUT THIS JUST ISN'T TRUE! *BASIC ECONOMIC PRINCIPLES DO* **NOT** *CHANGE WITH THE* **SIZE** OF AN ECONOMY... THEY'RE JUST HARDER TO *SEE* BECAUSE OF MORE COMPLICATED AGENCIES...
...AND TERMINOLOGY. DIRECT RELATIONSHIP BETWEEN SELF SACRIFICE, SAVINGS, CREDIT, INVESTMENT, ECONOMIC INCENTIVE, SOCIAL AND ECONOMIC PROGRESS IS ALWAYS THE SAME!
SIMILARLY, THE **PRINCIPLES** OF **MATH** DON'T CHANGE WITH THE **SIZE** OF THE PROBLEMS...
*IT'S* **STILL ADDITION!**
1 +1 2
Ledger:
1,302,689.10
3,091.60
750,981.03
3,172,262.00
18.19
+ 568,906.21
5,797,948.13

# GOVERNMENT on the ISLAND

SELF GOVERNMENT WAS THE BOTTOM LINE...
I MIND MY OWN! EVERYBODY ELSE DO LIKEWISE... OR ELSE!
KEEP OUT
SETTLING DISPUTES AND CRIMES OF PASSION HAD LONG BEEN SETTLED BY THE ISLANDERS IN A VERY DIRECT AND PERSONAL MANNER...
C'MON, PAW... UNCLE NED! THE VARMINT STOLE OUR HEN!
GO GIT HIM BOYS!
THIS CONTRACT IS VOID!
RIP! RIP! RIP! RIP!
YOU CAN'T DO THAT!
CAN YOU?
STICK 'EM UP!
HELP, SOMEBODY! P-PLEASE!
BUT SELDOM WAS THERE ANY HELP AROUND!

THE ISLANDERS DECIDED TO ELECT A SENATE TO SELECT AND OVERSEE JUDGES AND A CONSTABULARY, WHOSE PURPOSE WAS TO PROTECT LIFE, RIGHTS AND PROPERTY...
LET'S ELECT 12 SENATORS TO DO THE JOB!
C'MON! EVERYBODY GET OUT AND VOTE!
HOLD IT! LET'S DECIDE ON A VOLUNTARY VOTING TAX!
PAY TO VOTE?! HOW UNDEMOCRATIC! IT SHOULD BE FREE!
INDEED?
BUT IF A VOTE COSTS NOTHING IT'S WORTH NOTHING!
THE IGNORANT AND IRRESPONSIBLE WILL VOTE IF IT'S FREE, AND SUCH VOTES ARE DANGEROUS!
I LIKE THE WAY THIS CANDIDATE PARTS HIS HAIR!
ELECT
FREEWILL TO SENATE
EENIE, MEANIE, MINEY, MOE...ONE'S AS GOOD AS ANOTHER!
VOTE 4
GRINSTED

IN GOVERNMENT IF YOU WANT A SAY, THEN YOU'VE GOT TO PAY!
OKAY!
IT'LL HELP DEFRAY THE COSTS OF GOVERNMENT, TOO!
VOTE (5 FISH)
BALLOT BOX
LET THE STUPID and WHO-CARES CITIZEN STAY HOME! IF HE PAYS TO VOTE HE'LL PAY MORE ATTENTION TO THE ISSUES AND THE CANDIDATES...
HOLD IT! MR. GOLDSMITH IS RICH... HE SHOULD PAY MORE TO VOTE!
WHY IS THAT?
BALLOT BOX
RICH AND POOR ALIKE WILL RECEIVE THE SAME BENEFITS FROM GOVERNMENT ... PROTECTION OF LIFE, LIBERTY, AND PROPERTY!
LIKE GOING TO THE THEATER...THE PRICE IS THE SAME FOR EVERYBODY...EACH PERSON ENJOYS THE SAME ENTERTAINMENT...

OKAY...YOU WIN AGAIN, MR. JUSTICE ...EVERYBODY SHOULD PAY THE SAME TAX TO VOTE!
VOTE (5 FISH)
BALLOT BOX
HUH? LOOK WHO'S COMING TO VOTE!
HOLD IT, SONNY!
HUH?
YOU'RE TOO YOUNG TO VOTE!
WHAT DOES AGE HAVE TO DO WITH IT?
VOTE (5 FISH)
BALLOT BOX
I WORK! I'M A PRODUCTIVE MEMBER OF SOCIETY, AND I'LL PAY THE 5 FISH TAX TO VOTE!
ER... UM... YOU'VE GOT ME THERE, KID!
ON THE OTHER HAND, THAT OLD HOBO CONTRIBUTES ZERO TO OUR SOCIETY AND HIS JUDGMENT IS QUESTIONABLE!
LOT

WHY PAY TO VOTE?
SO I CAN HAVE A SAY IN WHAT KIND OF MEN ARE ELECTED!
5 FISH IS A CHEAP PRICE TO PAY FOR CONTROL OF ECONOMIC AND SOCIAL JUSTICE!

SOME OF THE ISLANDERS, OF COURSE, WOULD NOT HAVE GIVEN EVEN **ONE** FISH LET ALONE **FIVE**, TO PROMOTE ECONOMIC AND SOCIAL JUSTICE! FORTUNATELY, THEY DID ***NOT*** HAVE A VOICE IN THE ISLAND'S GOVERNMENT!
WHO CARES?!

AND SO, WITH THE ENFORCEMENT OF **JUST LAWS**, AND THE **COURT SYSTEM** ENFORCING CONTRACTS AND DISPUTES AMONG TRADESMEN, TRADE WAS FACILITATED, AND THIS FURTHER INCREASED THE DIVISION OF LABOR, INCREASING ECONOMIC BENEFITS FOR **ALL**...TAXPAYERS AND NON TAXPAYERS ALIKE!
THE ISLAND'S ECONOMY CONTINUED TO GROW, AND *EVERYBODY PROSPERED!*

DEMOCRACY
REARS ITS UGLY HEAD
A FEW MORE GENERATIONS PASS, AND THE POLITICAL COMPLEXION OF THE ISLAND HAS CHANGED! IN A BURST OF DEMOCRATIC FERVER EVERY ONE ON THE ISLAND HAS BEEN GIVEN THE VOTE!
VOTE
VOTER'S BUS
SENATORS ARE NOW HIGHLY PAID INDIVIDUALS, WHO SEEK OFFICE MORE FOR MONEY AND POWER THAN FOR THE HONOR OF DISPENSING JUSTICE...
Senate Seat
MANY OF THEM SPEND SMALL FORTUNES TO GET ELECTED!

SENATORS ALSO "PAY" THEIR WAY INTO OFFICE BY DISPENSING FAVORS WHICH WIN VOTES!
FRIENDS, WELFARITES, AND FAVOR-SEEKERS...
SPLAT!
FISHPALM for SENATE
H-HEY... WHAT ABOUT ME?
DISPENSING FAVORS WINS VOTES DISPENSING JUSTICE DOES NOT!
(BY THE NEW DEMOCRATIC THINKOLOGY)
FAVORS OF ALL FLAVORS
LAW
VOTERS
SUCH IS THE REALITY OF POLITICAL LIFE ON the ISLAND NOW!

# the Courts

THE COURTS STILL THEORETICALLY DISPENSED JUSTICE, BUT THE QUALITY OF JUSTICE HAD SUFFERED BECAUSE OF THE KIND OF JUDGES THE SENATORS WERE NOW APPOINTING!

YOU'RE A GOOD PARTY MAN, GORMAN GAVEL... YOU'RE **IN**!
YOU CAN COUNT ON ME, OL' BUDDY!

WORSE YET, THE **LEGITIMATE COURTS** WERE REPLACED BY A HOST OF **NEW ADMINISTRATIVE COURTS** SET UP BY THE SENATE TO ADMINISTER A QUAGMIRE OF NEW LAWS THEY HAD PASSED! THESE COURTS FUNCTION ***OUTSIDE*** THE ***REAL*** LEGAL SYSTEM AND ARE CONTROLLED BY THE SENATE!
WHAT CONSTITUTIONAL RIGHTS?!
GUILTY!
**PROVE** YOU'RE INNOCENT!
TAX CO
BUREAUCOURT
COURT-OF-NO-APPEAL
KANGAROO ROW
ADM RUL

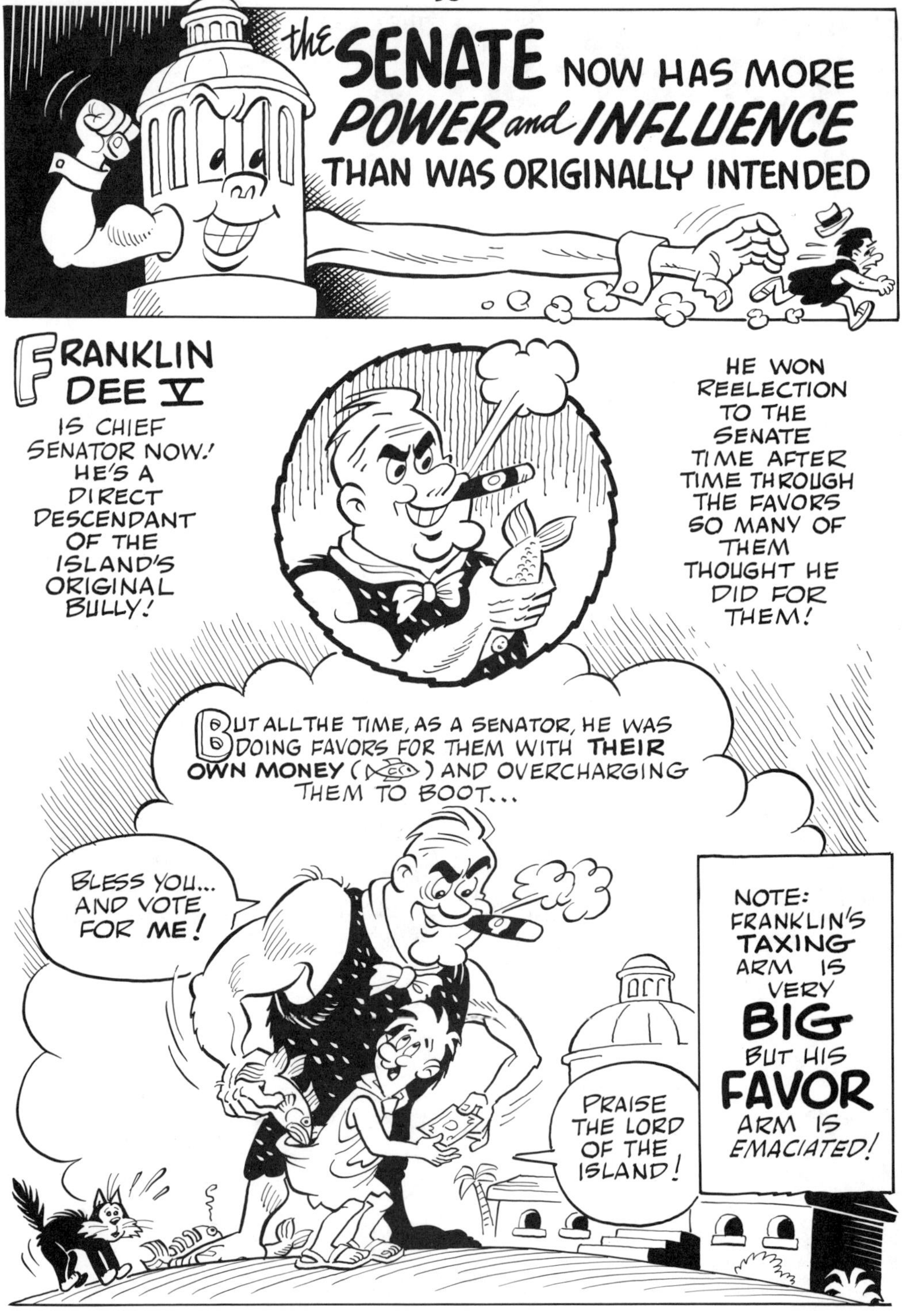
the SENATE NOW HAS MORE POWER and INFLUENCE THAN WAS ORIGINALLY INTENDED
FRANKLIN DEE V IS CHIEF SENATOR NOW! HE'S A DIRECT DESCENDANT OF THE ISLAND'S ORIGINAL BULLY!
HE WON REELECTION TO THE SENATE TIME AFTER TIME THROUGH THE FAVORS SO MANY OF THEM THOUGHT HE DID FOR THEM!
BUT ALL THE TIME, AS A SENATOR, HE WAS DOING FAVORS FOR THEM WITH THEIR OWN MONEY ( ) AND OVERCHARGING THEM TO BOOT...
BLESS YOU... AND VOTE FOR ME!
PRAISE THE LORD OF THE ISLAND!
NOTE: FRANKLIN'S TAXING ARM IS VERY BIG BUT HIS FAVOR ARM IS EMACIATED!

NOW FRANKLIN WAS ALWAYS LOOKING FOR NEW WAYS TO BESTOW VOTE-GETTING FAVORS TO KEEP HIMSELF IN OFFICE...
HMMM HMMM!
THINK TANK
HMMMM...THE NEW DIRECTOR OF THE BANK, SEYMOUR GOODBANK, A DIRECT DESCENDANT OF MAX GOODBANK, THE BANK'S FOUNDER, IS REJECTING A NUMBER OF REQUESTS FOR COMMERCIAL AND CONSUMPTION LOANS! THERE MUST BE A WAY TO USE THESE REJECTED LOAN APPLICANTS! HMMM...
SORRY! I'M A CONSCIENTIOUS GUARDIAN OF THE ISLAND'S SAVINGS!
STINGY!
BAH!
TIGHTWAD!

POW!
FRANKLIN HAD A BUREAUCRATIC BRAINSTORM...
ZAP!
AND THE SENATE PASSED A NEW LAW...
E-Z TO GET GOV'T LOAN LOW INTEREST
NEW LAW
BUSINESS
HOUSING
SCHOOL
FARM
WOMEN
NOW JUST ABOUT EVERY TOM, DRIP, AND HARRY COULD GET A GOVERNMENT LOAN...AND THE SENATORS HAD BOUGHT ANOTHER BIG BLOCK OF VOTERS!
BUT JUST WHOSE FISH-MONEY IS BEING LOANED OUT ?

THE GOVERNMENT DOESN'T POSSESS EVEN A PIGGY BANK OF SAVINGS!
YOU GUESSED IT...GOVERNMENT LOANS REALLY COME FROM TAXING SOCIETY'S PRODUCERS, HENCE REDUCING WHAT THEY CAN SAVE, AND DIMINISHING THE ISLAND'S LIMITED SUPPLY OF SAVINGS FOR SOUND INVESTMENTS!
TAX
BANK
NOW THAT EVERY ONE VOTES...EVERY ONE ALSO HAS TO PAY TAXES!

BUT MOST OF GOVERNMENT LOANS WERE MADE IN A MORE SNEAKY AND INDIRECT WAY! THE GOVERNMENT ISSUED BIG BATCHES OF FRANKLIN RESERVE NOTES!
ALL I NEED IS PAPER AND INK TO MAKE LOANS!
HUH? WHAT DO WE DO WITH THESE PIECES OF PAPER?
FRANKLIN RESERVE NOTE
PAY TO THE BEARER ON DEMAND
TEN FISH

WHY, JUST RUN DOWN TO THE BANK WITH YOUR "FRANKLIN RESERVE NOTES" AND TURN THEM IN FOR FISH!
GOV'T LOANS
NEAT!
(GROAN!) WHAT CAN I DO? THEY MADE IT A LAW!
WALK UP WINDOW

NOW A **SAVER'S** CLAIM TO FISH HE HAD ***WORKED FOR*** AND DEPOSITED AS EVIDENCED BY HIS ***DEPOSIT BOOK,*** WAS NO BETTER CLAIM TO HIS PRODUCTIVITY THAN WHAT COULD BE WITHDRAWN WITH **FRANKLIN RESERVE NOTES...**

WORK
SAVINGS PASS BOOK
THIS IS EQUALITY?
NO SWEAT GOV'T LOAN

THUS, THE GOVERNMENT PROVIDED PRODUCERS AND NON-PRODUCERS ALIKE WITH THE SAME "DEMOCRATIC" ACCESS TO THE COMMUNITY'S STORE OF SAVINGS!

BUT NO MATTER HOW YOU SLICE IT ...WHETHER A MAN'S PROPERTY IS TAKEN BY A THUG OR BY A FUNNY MONEY SCHEME IT'S STILL CALLED THEFT!
LET BIG BROTHER DO IT!
GOV'T LOANS
...THE ONLY DIFFERENCE BEING THAT SOME THIEVES LET THE GOVERNMENT DO THEIR DIRTY WORK FOR THEM!
BUT EVENTUALLY EVEN THOSE WHO CLAIM FAVORS FROM GOVERNMENT REALIZE THAT GOVERNMENT'S BITE IS BIGGER THAN ITS BENEVOLENCE!
IT TAKES A LOT JUST TO KEEP MY MACHINERY RUNNING!
SCHLOORP!

WHEN THE IDEA FOR A FRANKLIN RESERVE SYSTEM WAS FIRST PROPOSED TO MR. GOODBANK, HE VIGOROUSLY OPPOSED IT, AND SO THE SENATORS AGREED TO WIELD THEIR CREDIT POWER JUDICIOUSLY! BESIDES, THE GREEDY VOTERS AND POWERFUL SENATE WERE AN IRRESISTIBLE FORCE, AND THE LAW WAS PASSED!
PRESSURE FROM ABOVE
and
PRESSURE FROM BELOW
the SENATE
the VOTERS
FLAP!
PROMISES
FLAP!
FLAP!
FLAP!
E-Z GOV'T LOANS
BUT AFTER THE LAW WAS PASSED, IT WAS SOON AMENDED TO REMOVE RESTRICTIVE PASSAGES, AND PROMISES OF GOVERNMENT'S RESPONSIBLE USE OF CREDIT WERE SOON FORGOTTEN!
AND SO, AT THE END OF THE FIRST YEAR, A LARGE VOLUME OF FISH HAD BEEN WITHDRAWN FROM THE BANK BY MEANS OF FRANKLIN RESERVE NOTES...
TH-THIS IS DISASTROUS!
AVINGS

INSTEAD OF THE SAVERS HAVING A PROFIT THIS YEAR, THEY'VE SUFFERED A LOSS!
NOW I CAN RETURN ONLY 9 FISH FOR EVERY 10 PUT IN!
HUH?!
10
9
IF THE SAVERS FIND OUT THEY MAY WITH-DRAW THEIR FISH AND QUIT USING MY BANK!
ZERO
SO MONEY-BAGS IS OUT OF BUSINESS! SO WHAT? WHO CARES?
EVERYBODY SHOULD CARE, SIR! THE WHOLE ISLAND IS DEPENDANT UPON SAVINGS!

SO? PEOPLE WILL JUST SAVE THEIR FISH AT HOME, MONEYBAGS!
SEE HERE, MR. FORGETFUL... THAT WILL PUT US BACK MANY YEARS! THERE WILL BE NO POOL OF CAPITAL AVAILABLE TO MAINTAIN THE CAPITAL EQUIPMENT WE NOW RELY ON, MUCH LESS CAPITAL FOR NEW PROJECTS!
BUS STOP
BUS

GOODBANK WAS THINKING OF THE WATERWORKS, NOW GREATLY EXPANDED TO FURNISH WATER TO THE REMOTEST CORNER OF THE ISLAND...
THE WATERWORKS NOW EMPLOYED 150 WORKERS TO MAINTAIN ITS SYSTEM! IT TOOK 54,750 FISH A YEAR JUST TO FEED THEM. IF SAVERS QUIT SAVING FISH AT THE BANK THERE WOULD BE NO WAY TO FEED THE WATERWORK'S WORKERS!
WATER-WORKS

THEN THERE ARE MAINTENANCE AND REPAIR COSTS...
SPLAT!
IF ALL THE WORKERS WALKED OFF THE JOB TO FISH FOR A LIVING AGAIN...
...THE WATERWORKS WOULD FINALLY QUIT WORKING!
SOAP

AND THE ISLAND'S ENTIRE ECONOMY WOULD BE IN BIG TROUBLE AS PEOPLE WOULD HAVE TO RELOCATE NEAR ACCESSIBLE WATER AGAIN...
BACK TO THE OLD BUCKET TOTING AGAIN!
UGH!
I HAVEN'T FOUND A NEW JOB YET!
ME FOR HIRE
I CAN'T LET THAT HAPPEN!
SENATOR! SENATOR!
SENATOR FRANKLIN DEE
BAM!
BAM!
GOODBANK SPILLS HIS TROUBLES TO FRANKLIN...

ONCE THE SAVERS ON THE ISLAND REALIZE THAT THEY ARE **LOSING** THEIR SAVINGS STORED AT MY BANK THEY WILL STOP SAVING! YOU WILL THEN SEE OUR WHOLE ECONOMY COLLAPSE... LIKE WATCHING AN EARTHQUAKE IN SLOW MOTION!
HIGH TOP BUILDING

DON'T GET SO EXCITED, GOODBANK! WHY SHOULD THE SAVERS HAVE TO KNOW THAT THEIR SAVINGS ARE SHRINKING AND NOT GROWING?
WHY, IT'S NOW DECEMBER! IN A FEW WEEKS I'LL BE GIVING ALL DEPOSITORS THEIR ANNUAL STATEMENTS. INSTEAD OF HAVING THE USUAL 12 TO 13 FISH PER 10 SAVED, EACH DEPOSITOR WILL ONLY HAVE 8 OR 9!

TUT-TUT, GOODBANK! WE OF THE SENATE ARE FORESIGHTED...WE'LL FIX IT SO THE SAVERS CAN'T TELL THEY'RE COMING OUT SHORT!
BRING ON THE FISH TECHNICIANS!
FISH LAB
LOOK! WE'VE BEEN COLLECTING DISCARDED FISH SKINS AND SKELETAL REMAINS WITH HEAD AND TAIL!
FISH LA
NOW LET'S OPEN UP A GENUINE DRIED FISH!
PLOP!
SCAPEL...FISH GLUE...ACTION!
WH-WHAT'S GOING ON?
THEY'RE TAKING SOME OF THE MEAT FROM THE GENUINE DRIED FISH AND PUTTING IT AROUND A SKELETON AND COVERING IT WITH AN OLD FISH SKIN!

...AND PRESTO! WHAT WAS ONCE GARBAGE NOW LOOKS LIKE A GENUINE FISH! NOW WE HAVE TWO FISH!
AMAZING!
WE'LL USE THESE "OFFICIAL FISH" FOR MONEY, AND THE DEPOSITORS...
THE DEPOSITORS WILL GET WISE!
SEE? YOUR "OFFICIAL FISH" LOOK SKIMPY NEXT TO A GENUINE DRIED FISH!
OFFICIAL FISH NEED NOT BE THAT SMALL. WE'LL MAKE 5 OFFICIAL ONES OUT OF EVERY 4 REAL ONES, SO THEY'LL ONLY BE 20% SMALLER. IN ADDITION, WE'LL PASS A LAW TO PREVENT ISLANDERS FROM COMPARING THEM TO REAL FISH!
YES, PASS A LAW!

WE'LL SAY OUR SCIENTISTS HAVE DISCOVERED THE DREAD "POLUTYOO DISEASE" IN FISH, AND WE'LL REQUIRE EVERYONE TO TURN IN THEIR GENUINE FISH FOR OFFICIALLY DECONTAMINATED FISH!
THE DECONTAMINATION PROCESS WILL HELP EXPLAIN WHY "OFFICIAL FISH" LOOK A LITTLE FUNNY!
FOR SOCIETY'S PROTECTION, ANY ISLANDER CAUGHT STORING, SELLING, OR EATING "CONTAMINATED" UNOFFICIAL FISH WILL BE PUNISHED, FINED, AND IMPRISONED!
FISH TECH.
ALSO... IT'LL BE AGAINST THE LAW FOR ANYONE BUT AN "OFFICIAL FISHER" TO CATCH FISH FROM THE SEA!
NO FISHING ALLOWED!
SENATE LAW NO. 666
THIS MEANS YOU!

YOU'LL NEED LOTS OF UNDAMAGED FISH REMAINS TO MAKE THIS OPERATION WORK, SENATOR DEE!
WE'LL MERELY PASS ANOTHER TAX! IN ADDITION TO HIS REGULAR FISH TAX, EACH CITIZEN WILL BE REQUIRED TO PAY A TAX OF 365 FISH CARCASSES AND SKINS PER YEAR!
WHY WOULD CITIZENS TURN IN THEIR FISH CARCASSES AND SKINS IN GOOD CONDITION?
WE'LL TELL THEM THAT TO PREVENT POLLUTION ALL FISH REMAINS WILL BE PROCESSED THROUGH OUR SPECIAL DISPOSAL SYSTEM...
...AND THAT ONLY REMAINS IN GOOD CON-DITION CAN PASS THROUGH OUR EQUIPMENT. NO ONE WILL GET TAX CREDIT FOR REMAINS TURNED IN IN POOR CARCASS CONDITION!
BUT WAIT...IN THE LONG RUN THIS WON'T WORK! EVENTUALLY THE REAL FISH SUPPLY NEEDED TO SUPPORT CONSUMPTION REQUIRE-MENTS FOR CAPITAL REPLACE-MENT AND GROWTH WILL DISAPPEAR!
SENATE CHAMBER
"THE WHOLE ECONOMIC STRUCTURE OF THE ISLAND WILL COLLAPSE", POINTED OUT GOODBANK!

WE KNOW! BUT IT WILL WORK TILL AFTER THE NEXT ELECTION! WE CAN WORRY ABOUT IT THEN!
MEANWHILE, GOODBANK... THIS WILL GIVE YOU ENOUGH "OFFICIAL FISH" TO PAY THIS YEAR'S INTEREST... ONE FISH EARNED FOR EVERY TEN FISH SAVED!
SEN. RICHARD TRICKSON
SEN. LYNDON B. SWANSON
THIS SCHEME WILL ENABLE US TO ESTABLISH A "GREAT SOCIETY"!
SEN. HUBERT HUMPTY
WELL, SEYMOUR GOODBANK, YOU WILL GO ALONG WITH THIS, WON'T YOU?
ABSOLUTELY NO! IT'S FRAUD... DECEPTION...
I WAS AFRAID OF THIS!

"GREAT SOCIETY," INDEED! IT WOULD BE A GREAT SWINDLE! IF THERE'S ONE TRAIT YOU SENATORS HAVE IN COMMON IT'S DISHONESTY! I'LL CLOSE THE BANK AND TELL THE PEOPLE TO SAVE THEIR FISH AT HOME BEFORE I GO ALONG WITH...
WE'VE HEARD ENOUGH!
GUARDS!
GOODBANK'S PARTING WORDS FALL ON DEAF EARS...
GET CHESLEY BARTIN IN HERE!
THIEVES! MURDERERS!
CHESLEY, YOU'RE THE NEW DIRECTOR OF FISHBANK...ER, UNDER OUR SUPERVISION!
WHERE'S MY RUBBER STAMP, SENATORS?

WHY, IT...IT'S SEYMOUR GOODBANK'S BODY!
YES, AND IT'S PLAIN TO SEE THAT HE DIED OF NATURAL CAUSES!
EULOGIES WASHED WITH CROCODILE TEARS ARE OFFERED...
ELECT SEN. DEE
WE'LL HAVE A SPECTACULAR FUNERAL!
BUT HOW COULD THE ISLANDERS HAVE KNOWN THAT NOT ONLY HAD THEY BURIED GOODBANK, BUT THE ISLAND'S TRADITION FOR HONEST BANKING AS WELL!
SEYMOUR GOODBANK

CHESLEY BARTIN NOW EXECUTED FRANKLIN DEE'S SCHEME, AND IT WORKED...THE TRANSITION FROM GENUINE FISH TO "OFFICIAL FISH" WAS MADE...
THE ISLANDERS NEVER SUSPECTED THE DISHONEST RELATIONSHIP BETWEEN THEIR SENATORS AND THE BANKER...

BUT AS TIME PASSED MANY MORE FRANKLIN RESERVE NOTES WERE ISSUED SO MANY MORE "OFFICIAL FISH" HAD TO BE MADE FROM REAL ONES. OFFICIAL FISH BECAME SMALLER AND SMALLER...

EVENTUALLY "OFFICIAL FISH" WERE *HALF THE SIZE OF* REAL FISH. AS A RESULT, THE ISLANDERS NOW CONSUMED TWO FISH A DAY INSTEAD OF ONE...

A **DOUBLE** BLUE PLATE SPECIAL PLEASE!

PRICES, WHICH HAD BEEN GEARED TO THE ISLANDERS' DAILY FISH CONSUMPTION, WERE NOW **DOUBLE** WHAT THEY HAD BEEN BEFORE "FRANKLIN RESERVE NOTES" HAD BEEN INTRODUCED...
*WHY ARE PRICES GOING UP?*
INFLATION!
SALE
~~10 FISH~~
20 FISH
MEN'S WEAR

# INFLATIONS' CAUSE

WALTER WHICKEL, A LOCAL FISH MERCHANT AND THE ISLAND'S PART TIME ECONOMIST HAD A THEORY...
INFLATION IS CAUSED BY A "COST-PRICE FISH-PUSH"!
WE CAN STIMULATE THE ECONOMY BY HOLDING DOWN PRICE INCREASES TO ABOUT HALF A BELLY A YEAR!
FISH
THE GOVERNMENT BUBBLED OVER WITH EXPLANATIONS...
PRICES HAVE GONE UP BECAUSE WE'RE SO PROSPEROUS!
YOU'RE DEMANDING MORE AND SPENDING MORE!
WHY, YOU'RE CONSUMING TWICE WHAT YOUR FOREFATHERS DID!
AND YOU'RE WASTEFUL!
INFLATION IS IS MERELY THE PRICE OF PROSPERITY!
BUT NOBODY THOUGHT OF POINTING A FINGER AT GOVERNMENT, THE REAL CAUSE OF INFLATION!

SINCE OFFICIAL FISH WERE NOW SO MUCH SMALLER THAN NORMAL FISH, THE GOVERNMENT WAS FORCED TO PASS YET ANOTHER LAW.

WE HAD BETTER DO SOMETHING TO PREVENT FISHERMEN FROM NOTICING HOW LARGE *REAL FISH* ARE!
I'M ONE STEP AHEAD OF YOU ON *THAT* ONE! WE'LL SAY THAT OUR SCIENTISTS DISCOVERED THAT FISH TAKEN DIRECTLY FROM THE SEA EMIT *HARMFUL RADIATION!* TO PROTECT THEIR EYES, *"OFFICIAL FISHERMEN" WILL BE REQUIRED TO WEAR THESE SPECIAL "FISH GLASSES!"*
THIS WAY WE CAN KEEP OUR SCAM GOING INDEFINITELY!

IN ADDITION, TO ASSURE THE ISLANDERS THAT THEIR FISH WERE SAFE IN THE BANK, THE GOVERNMENT CREATED THE

**FDIC...**

FISH DEPOSIT INSURANCE CORPORATION

THIS LAW WILL SHOW THE PUBLIC HOW *CONCERNED* WE ARE ABOUT THEIR SAVINGS!
YEAH, AND IF THEY THINK THEIR SAVINGS ARE INSURED, THEY WON'T NOTICE HOW THEY ARE **SHRINKING!**
Member FDIC

SO THE GOVERNMENT AND THE BANK CONTINUED TO MANUFACTURE SMALLER & SMALLER "OFFICIAL FISH"... AND MORE AND MORE "FRANKLIN RESERVE NOTES" WERE ISSUED! WAGES AND PRICES, THEREFORE, CONTINUED UP, UP, UP!
AND BY THE TIME "OFFICIAL FISH" WERE ONLY A THIRD THE SIZE OF NORMAL FISH, PRICES WERE UP 200 % FROM WHAT THEY HAD BEEN PRIOR TO THE CIRCULATION OF "FRANKLIN RESERVE NOTES"!
WAGES
PRICES
200% STRATOSPHERE

NOW YET ANOTHER LAW CONTROLLING "OFFICIAL FISHERMEN" WAS PASSED...
THEY MUSTN'T EVEN TOUCH REAL FISH!
STAMP!

THE NEW "FISHING REGULATIONS" PROHIBITED FISHERMEN FROM EMPTYING THEIR NETS...*ONLY GOVERNMENT "FISHING COORDINATORS"* COULD DO THAT... TO *PROMOTE THE GENERAL WELFARE...*

THE FISH DISEASE IS GETTING WORSE!
THERE'S ONLY ENOUGH IMMUNITY SERUM FOR US!
WE'LL RELIEVE YOU OF YOUR CATCH AND PAY YOU IN "FRANKLIN RESERVE NOTES"!
(SIGH!) I GUESS SO! IT'S THE LAW!
GOV'T

THIS WAY ONLY A SMALL GROUP OF "INSIDERS" ACTUALLY TOUCHED REAL, BIG, NORMAL FISH...
THE SENATE DOESN'T WANT THOSE DUMB SLOBS TO GET WISE TO THE "OFFICIAL FISH" SCAM!
FISH DEPTH
WHY SHOULD WE CARE? WE'VE GOT GOOD GOVERNMENT JOBS!

BUT YOU CAN'T FOOL ALL OF THE FISHERMEN ALL OF THE TIME! SOME DARING FISHERMEN DETECTED THE FRAUD...
LOOK, FRED... HOW FAT AND HEALTHY A REAL FISH IS!
IT'S MUCH HEAVIER THAN "OFFICIAL FISH" TOO!
THESE "LAWBREAKERS" WITHDREW THEIR "OFFICIAL FISH" SAVINGS FROM THE BANK...
B-BUT...THINK OF THE INTEREST YOU'LL LOSE!
HAH! YOUR INTEREST IS SMALLER THAN THE INFLATION RATE!
WE'LL DO BETTER TO SAVE THESE AND OUR CATCHES OF GENUINE FISH AT HOME!
WALK-UP WINDOW
F.D.I.C.
MORE AND MORE FISHERMEN PEEKED AND DECIDED TO KEEP the REAL FISH THEY CAUGHT, ETC....IT WAS A "CRIME-WAVE"!..

FEWER REAL FISH FOUND THEIR WAY INTO OFFICIAL CHANNELS AND A LIVELY BLACK MARKET IN REAL FISH DEVELOPED...
THE FISHERMEN AREN'T BRINGING FISH INTO PORT ANY MORE!
BUT THERE'S A LOT OF FISHY BUSINESS GOING ON SENATOR!
THIS HAS GOT TO STOP! WE'LL SEND OUT SWARMS OF SEARCH PARTIES!
THOSE "LAWBREAKERS" FOUND IN POSSESSION OF REAL FISH WERE PROSECUTED...
CAUGHT YOU RED SNAPPER-HANDED, BONY AND CLOD!
CRASH!
EEK!
CRIME DOESN'T PAY!
BUT THERE WERE OTHER "LEGAL" WAYS AROUND THE ANTI-FISH LAWS...

"OFFSHORE BANKING" OF REAL FISH BECAME POPULAR AMONG FISH-WISE CITIZENS...

DEPOSIT TO THE ACCOUNT OF ABLE, III !
HOW UNPATRIOTIC!
WE'LL PASS LAWS TO STOP THESE CRIMINALS! LAWS! LAWS! LAWS!
AND SO, THE "FOREIGN FISH CONTROL REGULATION, NO. 91-508" WAS PASSED BY THE SENATE...
YOU CAN IMAGINE HOW MUCH OUTFLOW OF FISH THIS LAW STOPPED!
ALL CRIMINALS, REPORT YOUR FOREIGN DEPOSITS HERE!
Z Z Z Z

THE SENATE PASSED STILL MORE LEGISLATION, SUPPOSEDLY TO APPREHEND CRIMINALS, AND NOW ISLANDERS LEAVING THE LAND TO TRAVEL ABROAD ARE TARGETED...

HALT! YOU CANT TAKE MORE THAN 10 OFFICIAL FISH OUT OF THE COUNTRY!
BUT IT'S OUR VACATION!
IT'S ALSO OUR MONEY!
EEK! NOW WH-WHAT'S THIS BEAST DOING!?
HEH! THAT'S "SNORT," OUR CURRENCY SNIFFER!
SNORT'S SNOOT IS TRAINED TO DETECT "FRANKLIN RESERVE NOTES"! YOU ALSO CANNOT TAKE MORE THAN 10 OF THEM OUT!
B-BUT WHY?
'CAUSE WE WANNA NAB SMUGGLERS AND COUNTERFEITERS WHO DEAL IN LARGE SUMS!
GOSH! WE SURE DON'T HAVE MUCH FREEDOM ANY MORE!
YES, PEOPLE-CONTROL IS WHAT IT'S ALL ABOUT! THE POLITICIANS DON'T WANT HONEST CITIZENS HEDGING AGAINST INFLATION BY INVESTING ABROAD! HOLDING A TIGHT REIN IS THE NAME OF THE GAME!

As official fish got smaller and smaller, it made more economic sense for real producers to spend more time hiding 1 fish than catching 7 real fish which they were compelled to turn into the government for "Franklin Reserve Notes."..
SMUGGLER PATROL
1 REAL FISH
7
"OFFICIAL FISH"
FRANKLIN RESERVE NOTE
PAY TO THE BEARER ON DEMAND
ONE FISH
Fewer and fewer fish were turned in to the bank and to Manny Fund, and so there was less and less available for capital loans...
FISH SAVINGS AND LOAN CO
A loan for a new venture? Are you kidding? There's not even enough for loaning to the water works for upkeep!
Then I can't build a new factory!

WAGES AND PRICES ARE NOW 600% HIGHER THAN THEY WERE BEFORE "FRANKLIN RESERVE NOTES" CAME INTO USE!
UP 600% WAGES and PRICES
SINCE "OFFICIAL FISH" WERE SO SMALL IT TOOK 7 OF THEM TO PROVIDE EACH ISLANDER WITH THE SAME NUTRITION AS ONE NATURAL OR REAL FISH!
Blue Plate Special
SINCE FISH DEPOSITED IN THE BANK WERE LOSING VALUE SO QUICKLY, ISLANDERS WERE ENCOURAGED TO SAVE LESS, WHILE MANY SIMPLY DISCONTINUED SAVING COMPLETELY. FISH HAD TO BE SPENT QUICKLY TO AVOID LOSSES DUE TO INCREASING PRICES...
FURNITU
10 FISH
15 FISH

UNEMPLOYMENT GREW IN ALL SECTORS OF THE ECONOMY, SINCE THERE WAS NOW LESS SAVINGS AVAILABLE TO INDUSTRY TO FINANCE ITS CAPITAL NEEDS!

SOS
SHUT DOWN
LAY OFF
THERE'S A LOT OF UNREST AMONG THOSE SLOBS, SENATOR!
HMM... THOSE "SLOBS" ARE ALSO "VOTERS"! THIS IS SERIOUS!
SO SENATOR DEE DIPPED INTO HIS THINK-TANK FOR A SOLUTION TO THE UNEMPLOYMENT PROBLEM...
HMMM!
THINK TANK

BINGO!
I'VE GOT ANOTHER BRAINSTORM!
"UNEMPLOYMENT INSURANCE" WILL SAVE THE DAY!
THINK TANK
CHESLEY! PRINT UP A PILE OF "FRANKLIN DEE NOTES"!
1 FOR YOU AND 2 FOR ME!
YES, THAT'S IT! WE'LL PAY THE UNEMPLOYED VOTERS WITH NEW NOTES! ALL WE NEED IS PAPER AND INK!
UNE
INS

AND THE UNEMPLOYED ("BOUGHT VOTERS") RUSH DOWN TO THE BANK TO REDEEM THEIR "FRANKLIN DEE NOTES" FOR WHAT LITTLE IS LEFT OF THE DWINDLING DEPOSITS OF OFFICIAL FISH...
UNEMPLOYMENT INSURANCE
FISH
LOAN
EEK! IT'S A RUN ON THE BANK!
THE VAULT WAS SOON PICKED BARE...
WE'VE GOT PLENTY OF SKELETONS...
...AND EMPTY FISH SKINS, SIR!

HERE! SEE WHAT YOU CAN PICK OFF THESE BONES!
B-BUT THIS IS A TEN FISH NOTE!
WHAT ABOUT ME?
HEY!
PLOP!
SHALL I WARM UP YOUR THINK TANK, MR. BARTIN?
NO, NO... THERE'S NO TIME FOR THAT NOW!
TANK
ALL I NEED IS ONE MORE PIECE OF PAPER AND SOME INK!
AND SO...
SOME HOLIDAY!
NO WORK!
AND NO MONEY!
CLOSED! BANK HOLIDAY

CHESLEY BARTIN MADE AN END RUN OVER TO THE SENATE BUILDING...
THE BANK'S OUT OF BOTH GENUINE AND "OFFICIAL FISH"! AND
THE DUMB SLOBS...I MEAN, "VOTERS," ARE ALL OUT OF JOINT!
!
OOOH! MY THINK TANK ONLY GIVES ME A HEADACHE NOW!
LET'S CALL IN OUR ECONOMIC ADVISERS!
HERE THEY ARE... WALTER HICKEL AND PAUL SIBLING!
GOOD!
QUICK...WHAT'S YOUR ADVICE IN THE PRESENT ECONOMIC CRISIS?

EXPAND CREDIT!
LOWER TAXES!
WHAT!?!
BUT CREDIT'S BEEN EXPANDED UNTIL THERE'S NOTHING LEFT TO EXPAND!
AND THERE'S NOTHING LEFT TO PAY TAXES WITH!
CAN'T YOU BIRDS DO ANY BETTER THAN THAT?
EH? A CHORUS OF DISCONTENT RISING FROM THE STREETS...
RUMBLE!
CRASH!
WE WANT JOBS!
WE NEED MONEY!

ER...OUR ECONOMISTS ARE WORKING ON A NEW PLAN NOW, FOLKS...
EXPAND CREDIT!
LOWER TAXES!
WHAT'S NEW ABOUT THAT !?!

BAH! THAT'S ALL THE ECONOMICS THOSE BIRDS KNOW!
RETIRE THEM TO THEIR CAGE ON CRACKERS AND SEEDS!
EXPAND CREDIT!
LOWER TAXES!

THE MORALLY AND MONETARILY BANKRUPT SENATORS ENTERED INTO A FUTILE DEBATE...
WHAT ARE WE GOING TO DO?
WHAT CAN WE DO? ALL WE EVER DID WAS STEAL THE PEOPLE'S STORE OF SAVINGS TO FINANCE OUR VARIOUS PROJECTS!
NOW THERE ARE NO MORE SAVINGS TO STEAL!
JACK KASSIDY
FRANKLIN DEE
BUT WHY DON'T WE JUST CREATE JOBS FOR THE UNEMPLOYED?
"REMEMBER THE W.D.A. PROJECT OF GOOD OLD FRANKLIN DEE? WE EMPLOYED LOTS OF PEOPLE WASHING AWAY DIRT... CLEANING THE ROCKS ON THE BEACH!"
SOAP

LET'S SIMPLY CREATE JOBS AGAIN!
HOW DENSE CAN YOU GET, KASSIDY... GOVERNMENT CREATES NOTHING!
ALL WE EVER DID WAS STEAL THE COMMUNITY STORE OF SAVINGS WITH TAXES AND "FRANKLIN RESERVE NOTES," AND DIVIDE UP THE LOOT AMONG THE VOTERS!
AFTER TAKING OUR OWN BIG CHUNK!
THEN HOW ARE WE GOING TO PAY OFF ALL THOSE BONDS THAT WE SOLD TO THE PEOPLE, TELLING THEM TO "INVEST IN THE ISLAND"?
WE CAN'T!
JACK KASSIDY
AND THE BONDS WE GAVE TO THE BANK IN EXCHANGE FOR THE "FRANKLIN RESERVE NOTES" WE DISTRIBUTED?
WE CAN'T PAY FOR ANYTHING!
GIVE US JOBS!
GIVE US MONEY!
CRASH!
(GROAN!) BUT THOSE STUPID VOTERS STILL BELIEVE IN US!
THIS IS AWFUL!

INTO YOUR THINK TANK, FRANKLIN... SAVE THE ISLAND WITH ANOTHER CON!
NO WAY, JACK! THERE ARE NO MORE FOXY FIXES TO PULL OFF! ALL WE'RE LEFT WITH NOW IS TRUTH!

AND THEN FRANKLIN DEE UTTERED THE ONLY HONEST WORDS OF HIS ENTIRE POLITICAL CAREER...
FRIENDS, ISLANDERS, COUNTRYMEN...I THINK THE TIME HAS NOW COME FOR ALL OF US TO START FISHING ...AND QUICKLY!

# YOU CAN BE A PROPHET

INTERFERENCE BY VOTE SEEKING POLITICIANS BRINGS ECONOMIC MAYHEM

BUSINESS CYCLES, RECESSIONS, DEPRESSIONS, AND INFLATION ARE MAN-MADE...ALWAYS PREDICTABLE, ALWAYS AVOIDABLE!

EXAMPLE...
GOVERNMENT BORROWS and TAXES TO FUND WELFARE PROGRAMS
LOANS
FISH

PRODUCTIVE WORKERS ARE PENALIZED BY HIGHER TAXES, WHILE UNPRODUCTIVE INDIVIDUALS ARE REWARDED WITH GOVERNMENT AID. NOT ONLY DO SUCH PROGRAMS REDUCE INCENTIVES FOR ALL, BUT THEY DRAW UPON SOCIETY'S LIMITED STORE OF SAVINGS NEEDED TO CREATE CAPITAL AND PROVIDE JOBS!

# EXAMPLE... MINIMUM WAGE LAW

LET'S HELP THE NATION'S YOUTH BY PASSING A MINIMUM WAGE LAW!
LAW
FISHGATE CO.
MINIMUM WAGE LAW
YIKES! THAT'S PRETTY STEEP PAY! MY *PROFIT MARGIN* WON'T ALLOW ME TO HIRE AS MANY AS I'D LIKE TO HIRE ...NOT AT **THIS** HIGH PAY!
SO I'LL ONLY HIRE A **FEW** OF THE BEST QUALIFIED, MOST EXPERIENCED, AND HARDEST WORKERS!
**I** GOT *FIRED!*
**I** NEVER EVEN GOT *HIRED!*

THUS THE NATION'S YOUTH IS ***NOT*** HELPED! THERE IS MORE *UNEMPLOYMENT* AND PRODUCTION COSTS ARE LIKELY *HIGHER!*

# CONSUMER CREDIT VS. COMMERCIAL CREDIT

CONSUMER CREDIT
WASTES CREDIT! WHEN CREDIT IS USED UP FOR CONSUMER GOODS THERE IS LESS CREDIT AVAILABLE FOR PRODUCTIVE COMMERCIAL PURPOSES AND IT LOWERS A SOCIETY'S STANDARD OF LIVING...
FISH SAVINGS AND LOAN CO
I WANT TO BORROW TO BUILD A FACTORY!
SORRY! IT'S ALL USED UP ON CHARGE ACCOUNTS AND THE LIKE!
I BORROW TO CONSUME!

COMMERCIAL CREDIT
INCREASES CONSUMER GOODS, SAVINGS, AND INVESTMENT CAPITAL... IT RAISES THE STANDARD OF LIVING...
I BORROWED TO PRODUCE!
MORE JOBS... MORE GOODS AT LOWER PRICES!
FISHGATE CO.
JOBS APPLY WITHIN

# TO LOAN OR NOT TO LOAN

DENNY DEADBEAT IS DENIED A LOAN AT THE BANK...
NO WAY! I CAN'T RISK LOANING THE DEPOSITORS' MONEY OUT TO THE LIKES OF YOU!
LOANS
BUT SINCE BUREAU-CRATS LOAN OUT OTHER PEOPLE'S MONEY THEY FACE NO PERSONAL RISK AND THUS LOANS ARE MADE FOR POLITICAL RATHER THAN ECONOMIC MERIT!
YOU POOR VOTER...ER, I MEAN SOUL! COME... WE'LL GUARANTEE A LOAN TO YOU!
SMALL BUSINESS ADMINISTRATION
LOANS
AND LATER, WHEN "GO-GET-EM" GETZ APPLIES FOR A LOAN...
B-BUT...
I'M TERRIBLY SORRY, MR. GETZ, BUT I'M SHORT ON FISH TO LOAN! I'VE HAD TO MAKE TOO MANY GOVERNMENT INSURED LOANS! (SIGH!)
LOANS

EXAMPLE...
SUPPOSE THE GOVERNMENT OUTLAWED BANK CREDIT TO FINANCE AUTOMOBILE PURCHASES (CONSUMER CREDIT)...
YIKES! I DON'T HAVE ENOUGH CASH TO BUY IT!
NO CREDIT! 1000 FISH
VERY FEW PEOPLE DO!
EVERYBODY AT THE AUTO AGENCY IS STARVING FOR LACK OF SALES...
NOTHING'S MOVING!
WHAT'RE YOU GOING TO DO, BOSS?
THERE'S ONLY ONE THING TO DO...
SLASH PRICES DRASTICALLY...OR WE'LL GO UNDER!

NOW WITH MY TRADE-IN PLUS MY SAVINGS... ALMOST!
YOU COULD SELL YOUR POOL TABLE!
PRICE SLASHED Only 500 FISH

*READJUSTMENTS WOULD TAKE PLACE ALL ALONG THE LINE...*

THE DEALERS WON'T TAKE ANY MORE HIGH PRICED CARS!
KLASSY CAR COMPANY
NO, THANKS!

INSIDE THE KLASSY CAR COMPANY ROLL BACKS TAKE PLACE...
WE CAN'T PAY THAT MUCH FOR LOGS ANY MORE!
TAKE A WAGE-CUT OR A LAY-OFF!
BUYER
PERSONNEL

THE WHOLE ECONOMY WOULD BE EFFECTED... EVERYTHING WOULD ADJUST DOWNWARD...
ROLL BACK PRICES...
SALE!
LOWER WAGES!
ROLL BACK PRICES...
SALE
LOWER WAGES!
WORKERS WOULD FIND THEMSELVES IN LOWER TAX BRACKETS!
TAX MAN
AND THEY WOULD HAVE MORE OF THEIR PAYCHECK LEFT TO BUY LOWER PRICED CONSUMER GOODS...
OUTBOARD DUCKS 1/2 OFF!
OLDER AND RETIRED CITIZENS ON FIXED INCOMES AND SAVINGS WOULD BE HELPED BY THE DOWNWARD SHIFT IN THE PRICE STRUCTURE...
WE CAN AFFORD TO LIVE LIKE HUMANS AGAIN!
LOOK! WE CAN EVEN AFFORD A NEW CAR NOW!

EVENTUALLY, JUST AS MANY, IF NOT *MORE* CARS WOULD BE SOLD FOR CASH...

IT'S GOOD TO REALLY **OWN** IT!
NO BIG PAYMENTS!
NO HIGH INTEREST!
AND THEY WOULD HAVE *MORE MONEY* FOR TRAVEL!
WHO WOULD BE HURT?

NOT LENDERS...

WE DO A **BIGGER COMMERCIAL CREDIT** BUSINESS NOW!
BANK
SOCIETY'S BIGGEST SPENDTHRIFT AND OVEREXTENDED DEBTOR, THE **GOVERNMENT** WOULD BE IN BIG TROUBLE...
TAX REVENUES ARE *DOWN* AND I OWE **TRILLIONS**!
**I'M** GOING TO HAVE TO *CUT-BACK*, TOO!
Bill

NOW YOU SEE WHY GOVERNMENT ENCOURAGES CONSUMER CREDIT... NOT TO BENEFIT THE CONSUMER, BUT TO **BENEFIT ITSELF!**

# finis

*But more examples follow...*

# *Reference Materials: Books, Reports, And Tapes By Irwin Schiff*

***BOOKS and REPORTS:***

***The Schiff Report***

An indispensible publication for those who want detailed instructions on how to protect themselves from the IRS. Provides information nowhere else available including documents, sample legal instruments, and procedures to use against the IRS. Many subscribers report that each issue is worth the price of the subscription. Also contains Irwin Schiff's economic and political commentary. 8 issues per year. Newsletter format, ∅75.00/Volume III subscription. Special offer: Volumes I, II, and III -∅150.00. Single issues, ∅10.00.

***The Great Income Tax Hoax,*** by Irwin Schiff

An unbelievable 573 page exposé of the entire Federal income tax and how the Federal Government has illegally collected this tax for over 70 years. Discover why the Supreme Court declared this tax unconstitutional and how the IRS disregards that decision, the 16th Amendment and the income tax laws themselves. Extensive material on the history of taxes, the illegal expansion of federal power and how to legally protect yourself from IRS harrassment. Fully documented. ∅18.00

***How Anyone Can Stop Paying Income Taxes***, by Irwin Schiff

Published in 1982, this book became the nation's best-selling hardcover book on Federal income taxes. Now in its fifth printing it has sold over 185,000 copies and neither the IRS nor any tax attorney has ever attempted to refute one word of it. It includes detailed instructions on how to stop paying income taxes, how to avoid audits and personal summonses, an analysis of the Privacy Act Notice, and much, much more. An indispensible companion to *The Great Income Tax Hoax*. Hardcover, ∅12.00

***The Social Security Swindle - How Anyone Can Drop Out***, by Irwin Schiff

An explosive exposé of Social Security - the biggest chain letter of them all. This book reveals in vivid detail all the underhanded practices employed by the Federal government to foist this swindle on the American public. It also provides readers with all the necessary documents and step-by-step procedures so that everyone (employees, employers, and self-employeds) can drop out of the social security scam. Hardcover, ∅13.00.

***The Biggest Con: How the Government Is Fleecing You***, by Irwin Schiff

With over 100,000 copies in print this book provides a complete and enjoyable education in economics and includes irrefutable evidence of the criminal and destructive nature of the Federal government. "The single most important book on the status of this nation I have ever read, " said Howard Ruff, editor of *The Ruff Times*. Softcover, ∅8.00.

***The Kingdom of Moltz***, by Irwin Schiff

A delightful tale of our monetary system written so that even a child of ten can understand it. "I laughed so hard I cried. Schiff's book is the greatest thing since sliced bread, " commented Dr. Camille Castorina, economics professor at St. Johns University. Softcover, ∅3.00.

**How An Economy Grows And Why It Doesn't**, by Irwin Schiff and Vic Lockman

While only 108 pages, this humorous, fully illustrated book provides readers with a thorough and fundamental understanding of what makes an economy grow and the reasons why it doesn't. Subjects include the causes of inflation; how capital is created, discouraged, and destroyed; and the use and misuse of commercial and consumer credit. A delightful political and economic satire. Softcover, ∅7.00

***AUDIO/VISUAL MATERIALS:***

1. Over the last eight years thousands of Americans have been enlightened and entertained by Irwin Schiff's famous Untax Seminars. His latest lecture is a series of three, one-hour video cassettes professionally filmed in Boston in 1984. Included is information on how not to pay Federal income and Social Security taxes as well as advanced techniques that can be used in fighting the IRS and the government.

Part I .......... ∅39.00
Part II .......... ∅39.00
Part III .......... ∅39.00
SPECIAL - all three parts .......... ∅99.00

**Please specify VHS or BETAMAX when ordering.**

2. New, 50 minute television show that was produced in Hollywood is now available. Suitable for airing on local/cable TV, it is also available on standard VHS or BETAMAX cassettes. An excellent educational tool, this show is also entertaining and will quickly convince viewers that no one is required to file Federal income taxes.

   50-Minute TV Special .................................... ∅75.00

   **Please specify VHS or BETAMAX when ordering. For Information and pricing on 1/4″ or 1/2″ tape for TV airing, contact FREEDOM BOOKS.**

3. Based on Irwin Schiff's *How Anyone Can Stop Paying Income Taxes,* these two, 90-minute audio tapes are convenient for use while driving or at home. An invaluable aid to those who are newcomers to the tax protest movement.

   Two Audio Tapes (C-90) ..................................∅15.00

***ALSO RECOMMENDED:***

***The Complete Internal Revenue Code***

The best weapon against the IRS is the law itself — in order to effectively fight the IRS each citizen should have a copy of the Internal Revenue Code since the IRS misleadingly states the law and attempts to confuse individuals regarding IRS regulations (which are not binding when they conflict with the law — as many of them do). Soft cover, ∅18.00.

***Handbook For Special Agents***

The Internal Revenue Service's handbook for its Criminal Investigation and Intelligence Divisions. Provides detailed information on the internal methods employed by the IRS in its illegal enforcement of the "income" tax. Softcover, ∅15.00. (the government charges ∅75.00 for this book.).

**Prices are denoted by ∅ which refers to Federal Reserve units — fiat currency now fraudulently circulating as U.S. dollars.**

**Please use the order form at the back of the book to order any of these materials.**

# ORDER FORM

**Quantity**

☐ **The Schiff Report, Volume III** ∅75.00
☐ The Schiff Report, Volumes I, II, and III ∅150.00
☐ The Schiff Report, Single Issue ∅10.00 (specify Vol. & No.)
☐ The Great Income Tax Hoax ∅18.00
☐ How Anyone Can Stop Paying Income Taxes ∅12.00
☐ The Social Security Swindle — How Anyone Can Drop Out ∅13.00
☐ The Biggest Con: How the Government Is Fleecing You ∅8.00
☐ The Tax Rebel's Guide to the Constitution and Declaration of Independence ∅2.50
☐ The Kingdom of Moltz ∅3.00
☐ How An Economy Grows And Why It Doesn't ∅7.00

AUDIO VISUAL MATERIALS: Please specify VHS or Betamax

Irwin Schiff's Untax Seminars — Video tapes

☐ Part I ∅39.00
☐ Part II ∅39.00
☐ Part III ∅39.00
☐ Special — all three parts ∅99.00
☐ 50-Minute TV Special ∅75.00
☐ Two Audio Tapes (C-90) ∅15.00

OTHER BOOKS AVAILABLE:

☐ The Complete Internal Revenue Code ∅18.00
☐ Handbook for Special Agents ∅20.00

*Please make check/money order payable to *Freedom Books* and mail to PO Box 5303, Hamden, Connecticut 06518.

NAME: ______________________________

ADDRESS: ______________________________
(street)

______________________________
(city) (state) (zip)

*For orders under ∅10.00 please add ∅1.00 for postage & handling.

## ORDER FORM

**Quantity**

☐ **The Schiff Report, Volume III** ∅75.00
☐ The Schiff Report, Volumes I, II, and III ∅150.00
☐ The Schiff Report, Single Issue ∅10.00 (specify Vol. & No.)
☐ The Great Income Tax Hoax ∅18.00
☐ How Anyone Can Stop Paying Income Taxes ∅12.00
☐ The Social Security Swindle — How Anyone Can Drop Out ∅13.00
☐ The Biggest Con: How the Government Is Fleecing You ∅8.00
☐ The Tax Rebel's Guide to the Constitution and Declaration of Independence ∅2.50
☐ The Kingdom of Moltz ∅3.00
☐ How An Economy Grows And Why It Doesn't ∅7.00

AUDIO VISUAL MATERIALS: Please specify VHS or Betamax

Irwin Schiff's Untax Seminars — Video tapes

☐ Part I ∅39.00
☐ Part II ∅39.00
☐ Part III ∅39.00
☐ Special — all three parts ∅99.00
☐ 50-Minute TV Special ∅75.00
☐ Two Audio Tapes (C-90) ∅15.00

OTHER BOOKS AVAILABLE:

☐ The Complete Internal Revenue Code ∅18.00
☐ Handbook for Special Agents ∅20.00

*Please make check/money order payable to *Freedom Books* and mail to PO Box 5303, Hamden, Connecticut 06518.

NAME: ______________________________

ADDRESS: ______________________________

(street)

______________________________

(city) (state) (zip)

*For orders under ∅10.00 please add ∅1.00 for postage & handling.

## ORDER FORM

**Quantity**

☐ **The Schiff Report, Volume III** ∅75.00
☐ The Schiff Report, Volumes I, II, and III ∅150.00
☐ The Schiff Report, Single Issue ∅10.00 (specify Vol. & No.)
☐ The Great Income Tax Hoax ∅18.00
☐ How Anyone Can Stop Paying Income Taxes ∅12.00
☐ The Social Security Swindle — How Anyone Can Drop Out ∅13.00
☐ The Biggest Con: How the Government Is Fleecing You ∅8.00
☐ The Tax Rebel's Guide to the Constitution and Declaration of Independence ∅2.50
☐ The Kingdom of Moltz ∅3.00
☐ How An Economy Grows And Why It Doesn't ∅7.00

AUDIO VISUAL MATERIALS: Please specify VHS or Betamax

Irwin Schiff's Untax Seminars — Video tapes

☐ Part I ∅39.00
☐ Part II ∅39.00
☐ Part III ∅39.00
☐ Special — all three parts ∅99.00
☐ 50-Minute TV Special ∅75.00
☐ Two Audio Tapes (C-90) ∅15.00

OTHER BOOKS AVAILABLE:

☐ The Complete Internal Revenue Code ∅18.00
☐ Handbook for Special Agents ∅20.00

*Please make check/money order payable to *Freedom Books* and mail to PO Box 5303, Hamden, Connecticut 06518.

NAME: ______________________________

ADDRESS: ______________________________
(street)

______________________________
(city) (state) (zip)

*For orders under ∅10.00 please add ∅1.00 for postage & handling.